LOLA MONTEZ

BETTMAN ARCHIVE

LOLA MONTEZ

Amanda Darling

STEIN AND DAY/*Publishers*/New York

First published in 1972

Library of Congress Catalog Card No. 74-185956

Published simultaneously in Canada by Saunders of Toronto, Ltd.
Designed by David Miller
Printed in the United States of America
Stein and Day/*Publishers*/7 East 48 Street, New York, N.Y. 10017
ISBN 0-8128-1436-3

Even my many enemies must admit
I always had a flair for living.
—Lola Montez, *Lectures*

A WORD TO THE READER

The unbridled imagination of Lola Montez creates as many pitfalls for her biographer as it does for the unwary reader, particularly where the first twenty-five years of Lola's life are concerned—before she became "the most infamous woman on earth," as British and American newspapers liked to call her. Lola, the sole authority for most details about her early life, tells her own story in her *Autobiography* and in the lectures she delivered in her last days, prior to the outbreak of the American Civil War. These distorted accounts, augmented by scores of newspaper interviews, are virtually the only available record of those years.

Lola had no respect for accuracy. Where prosaic fact might interfere with the dramatic, dim the luster of her glamour, or stand in the path of the flamboyant, she unhesitatingly discarded it for fiction.

In a sense, however, Lola's wild disregard for truth reveals more about her character than documented statistics would. Just as the psychiatrist of today finds the daydreams of his patient as significant as sleeping dreams, so Lola's reshaping of her past tells us far more than she realized about the forces that formed and motivated her.

I suggest that the reader adopt the approach that I was forced to take in the preparation of this book: when Lola herself is the sole authority for a fact, it should be accepted conditionally at best. As nearly as I can judge, she took the story of her early years a good deal less seriously than did her followers. Eventually, to be sure, she achieved such notoriety that she became the victim of her own publicity, and in time was no longer able to distinguish fact from fiction in her own mind.

What makes the sifting process so difficult is that Lola's real life was bizarre almost beyond belief: the real dramas in which she played a starring role frequently strain credulity. She would have been unique in any era, and living as she did at a time when Western civilization was more conservative and inhibited than ever before, she was regarded as a living wonder of the world.

Lola's beauty was her springboard to fame, a beauty that supposedly transcended changing standards; daguerreotypes taken a century and a quarter ago show her to be far less lovely to our eyes than she was said to be in her own time. But though she may have been ordinary in appearance, Lola had an extraordinary ability to create the *illusion* of beauty. Everyone who saw or knew her thought she was ravishing, and that alone mattered. In this sense, at least, she was an artist. Her "artistic" talents, even when judged leniently, were meager. As a dancer she was an international joke; her acting was worse than her dancing; her singing voice was nonexistent. Measuring Lola exclusively as an entertainer, there is no justification for her fame.

But Lola had qualities that have kept her name alive more than a century after her death. She was an independent spirit in an age when women were expected to be modest and retiring. Her ambitions exceeded those of most men, and she was as aggressive as she was imaginative about achieving them. Although she looked down her perfectly formed nose at the suffragettes who were her contemporaries, she was herself a prime mover—however unwittingly—in the campaign for women's rights. She led by example, breaking the rules of society with abandon and scorning the restrictions that hampered the activities of other members of her sex.

Her candor in allowing the world to see and share her pleasures was unique in her own time and rare in any age, and it was this that won her enduring fame. So it could be argued, perhaps, that in sacrificing facts to colorful drama Lola Montez did not distort the truth. The self-portraits she painted were photographic in their fidelity to the essence of her personality and to her spirit.

—A.D.

New York City

[CHAPTER I]

The fiction of Lola Montez' life begins at birth. Stripping that occasion of the romantic nonsense she later attributed to it, the most that can be said is that Maria Dolores Eliza Rosanna Gilbert—known from birth as Betty—was born in 1818, in Limerick, Ireland, where her father was stationed at the time.

Edward Gilbert was an ensign, or third lieutenant, in the 25th Regiment, known today as the King's Own Scottish Borderers. It is possible, as his only daughter later claimed, that he was the second son of a baronet and was descended from an old and distinguished family. No records substantiate this assertion. But the files of the War Office in London do disclose that Ensign Gilbert had risen from the ranks and had been awarded a commission because of valorous service in the field at the Battle of Waterloo. If Lola knew of this distinction, she made no mention of it when she wrote or spoke about her background.

Her mother was the former Marie, or Maria, Oliver, of "Castle Oliver," wherever and whatever that might have been. Lola is the only authority for the statement that Maria Oliver was the granddaughter of one Count de Montalvo, a Spanish grandee of Moorish descent who had lost his immense fortune in Napoleon's Peninsular Campaign.

It is reasonable to assume, in the light of Lola's four Christian names, that her mother was indeed of Spanish descent. Lola's many stories about her background changed from time to time, but she never varied from the statement that she was half Spanish, always attributing her femininity, charm, and "mystery" to the Spanish side of her family.

The pay of a very junior officer was small, and neither Ensign Gilbert nor his wife had a private income, so life must have been difficult for the young couple. But the Irish were even poorer, and the Gilberts were able to hire a nursemaid for their daughter. According to Lola, the nursemaid's terrifying stories about martyrs turned her against Roman Catholicism at a very early age.

In 1822 Gilbert's battalion was abolished, and Gilbert secured an appointment to the old 44th Regiment of the Line, now called the Essex Regiment, which was scheduled for immediate transfer to India.

Gilbert, his wife, and child spent only a few days in England, and when they reached the convoy of troop transports at Plymouth, the young officer found he had been promoted to the rank of second lieutenant. Second-guessers on board ship predicted that this would be the first of many promotions—the First Battalion, to which Lieutenant Gilbert had been assigned, had already reached India, and cholera, typhoid, and other diseases had decimated the ranks of her officers.

The voyage lasted more than four months, the convoy sailing around the southern tip of Africa only after crossing the Atlantic to make an unexplained stop at Rio de Janeiro. There were a number of children on the transport, but the most popular by far was pretty, lively Betty Gilbert, or so the grown-up Lola Montez later declared. In any event, the ships reached Calcutta in late February of 1823, and the newcomers were given temporary quarters at nearby Fort William. The regiment was ordered to take up its permanent station at Dinapore, located some hundreds of miles into the interior. All personnel, including the officers' dependents, were transferred there by flat-bottomed boats, which navigated India's rivers and ancient canals.

Lola remembered little of the tedious journey, but she never forgot the reception she and her mother were accorded at Dinapore. The officers and men of the First Battalion, starved for the sight of an attractive woman, spontaneously applauded when the lovely Mrs. Gilbert came down the gangplank. They cheered again when Betty was carried off the boat by her father; and one Captain John Craigie of the Bengal Army noted the frown that creased the mother's face.

Major General Brown, the commandant, mounted Betty Gilbert on his own horse to review the welcoming parade of the entire division. Not yet five years old, Betty had dark hair with deep, reddish glints, eyes of an arresting shade of blue, and the fresh, fair complexion that she would keep her entire life.

The garrison made a great fuss over the Gilberts, and every officer from the commandant down paid gallant court to the charming young wife and mother. Mrs. Gilbert was soon involved in a round of teas and dinners, luncheons and polo matches, and had little time to spare for her daughter. Lola was left in the company of native nursemaids and orderlies. At five she learned to ride and could handle both a pistol and a javelin; the nursemaids taught her Hindi and several local dialects, all of which she remembered as an adult. She spent most of her waking hours outdoors, and acquired a heavy tan under the Indian sun.

Betty was six when Lieutenant Gilbert was fatally stricken with cholera. On his deathbed he begged his good friend Captain Craigie to look after his widow and orphan.

After the funeral Major General and Mrs. Brown took Mrs. Gilbert and Betty under their own roof, but their guests did not remain with them long. The officers of the Indian Army looked after their own. Ladies were at a premium in the East, so the period of mourning for a late comrade-in-arms generally lasted no more than three months—after which time it was appropriate to sue for a widow's hand. A dozen officers watched the calendar, but Craigie, soon to be promoted to major, had the inside track. Precisely three months after Lieutenant Gilbert's death, his widow remarried.

John Craigie was a bluff, hearty man of enormous good will, with a strong sense of responsibility and a limited imagination. The new Mrs. Craigie immediately resumed the party life she loved, and Major Craigie, according to his correspondence with relatives in Scotland, was saddled with the task of providing his stepdaughter with an education. He taught her mathematics, Greek, and Latin himself, and she proved such an apt pupil that he also gave her courses in Portuguese and Spanish, languages he had acquired during the Peninsular War. He hired a junior officer to tutor her in English and other subjects.

Accustomed to having her own way, the little girl persuaded her young tutor to teach her bareback riding, and one day they were found on the range, where Betty was learning how to handle a cumbersome, long-barreled musket. Major Craigie was amused, but his wife was not—possibly because the story, which spread rapidly, made Betty the pet of every officer in the garrison.

In the early autumn of 1826, the Craigie family paid a visit to Calcutta, and at a formal levee Betty captivated the Viceroy, Lord William Bentinck, who made a place for her on his throne. She soon became the center of attention at the viceregal court.

Mrs. Craigie was growing tired of watching her daughter steal the spotlight. It wasn't long before Betty was shipped off to Scotland to her stepfather's family, presumably on the grounds that she could obtain a better education in Great Britain than in India. The mother's callousness left a strong impression on her child, who as a woman had no respect for the institution of motherhood.

The Craigie family lived in the damp, cold town of Montrose, a shipbuilding and fishing community built on the sand flats at the point where the South Esk River flows into the North Sea. The domestic atmosphere must have seemed as chilly as the climate to a child who was used to India. Old John Craigie, the head of the household, was a strict Calvinist, and so were the two spinster nieces who kept house for him. When Betty, undisciplined and spoiled, was catapulted into their household, there was strain on both sides.

Betty quickly developed an admiration for the old man. She

was sympathetic to the difficulties her presence created, an attitude she made clear many years later in her autobiography:

> This venerable man had been provost of Montrose for nearly a quarter of a century, and the dignity of his profession, as well as the great respectability of his family, made every event connected with his household a matter of some public note. So the arrived of the queer, wayward little East Indian girl was immediately known to all Montrose. The peculiarity of her light dress, and I dare say not a little eccentricity in her manners, served to make her an object of curiosity and remark; and very likely she perceived that she was somewhat of a public character, and may have begun, even at this early age, to assume airs and customs of her own.

What she did not record was how quickly "the queer little East Indian girl" won the battle. Her step-grandfather and his nieces soon adored her, making it possible for her to rule the household. She studied French, Spanish, and German, again showing her affinity for languages; she took courses in English grammar, rhetoric, and literature only because old Mr. Craigie insisted. She was also required to attend church services every Sunday morning without fail. As a result, she became strongly oriented toward Protestantism. Since there were virtually no Catholics in Montrose, and the Calvinist ministers of the town paid no attention to the few that were there, Lola's subsequent antipathy to the Church of Rome must have grown out of other causes.

During the four years spent with her stepfather's relatives, Betty exchanged regular, cordial letters with Major Craigie, but only at Christmas did she send her mother a dutiful note, receiving an equally stiff little communication in return. For all practical purposes, Mrs. Craigie had washed her hands of an unwanted daughter, and Betty had to live as best she could with the knowledge of this rejection. Years later, when she discovered that Balzac felt that he, too, had suffered because of his mother's indifference, she confided to him that she had solved her problem by pretending she was an orphan who had never known her mother.

When Betty was twelve, old Mr. Craigie suffered a severe illness that made it impractical to keep a growing child under his roof. His son, now Lieutenant Colonel Craigie, arranged for Betty to be taken into custody by his old friend, Major General Sir Jasper Nicolls, himself the father of two young daughters, who had just returned to England from India. Betty, sent down to London alone on a stagecoach, amused herself by sitting in the open beside the driver.

London, then a city of one and a half million, was a dazzling metropolis to Betty Gilbert. Sir Jasper and Lady Nicolls treated her with great kindness, and, with their own daughters also in tow, took her sightseeing everywhere. She saw palaces, churches, government buildings, and museums, but it was the theater and the smart restaurants that sparked her imagination.

"I fell hopelessly in love with the theatre," she wrote in her autobiography a quarter of a century later. "There I could escape from my own mean world into one of beauty and love and wealth."

Sir Jasper, a military hero of stature, had acquired a considerable fortune through his wife, and the Nicolls family moved in high circles. The pretty waif from India by way of Scotland was entertained at great houses in and out of London; there and in fine restaurants she watched the richly gowned and jeweled ladies who were pampered by important gentlemen. She was far more attractive than any of them, she confided to the Nicolls girls, but she would never permit any man to treat her like a delicate flower: she needed no one to help her dismount from a carriage or hold a door for her as though she were an invalid. The girls reported these observations to their parents, and Sir Jasper duly recorded them in his correspondence with Colonel Craigie.

Perhaps it was Betty's own idea to wear Indian dress when the Nicolls family went out to dinner or the theater, or perhaps her deep tan inspired Lady Nicolls to dress her in saris. Whoever was responsible, Betty created a sensation in her Eastern attire. And, in distant India, Mrs. Craigie learned that her daughter was becoming a beauty.

In 1831 Sir Jasper and Lady Nicolls decided to broaden the education of their daughters and their ward by taking all three to Paris for a year. There the new monarch, Louis Philippe, then known as the "citizen king," wore ordinary business attire as he walked to appointments daily through the streets of Paris.

Paris seemed a paradise to the thirteen-year-old Betty Gilbert, who stared at the gorgeously attired ladies she saw strolling on the boulevards or riding in their open coaches. She and the Nicolls girls were quickly put into a convent school operated by English nuns, where Betty had her first direct contact with Catholicism. She had been afraid of the sisters, but they treated her gently, and she even became their pet—perhaps because she could already speak, read, and write French fluently.

Whenever possible she worked on her tan, laughing at schoolmates who claimed the sun would make her old before her time. On weekends when she and the Nicolls girls returned to the custody of Sir Jasper, she continued to wear Indian attire, creating even more of a sensation in Paris than she had in London. Many people believed she really was an East Indian, despite her reddish hair and blue eyes, and she encouraged the deception by speaking only in Hindi when in their presence. By now her habit of escaping from reality by playing a role had become established and was assuming the proportions of a way of life rather than a game.

"Nothing gave me as much pleasure as pretending I was an East Indian, an English heiress or a Prussian princess," she would write. "These harmless deceptions helped me to forget that I was a nobody who had been abandoned by an indifferent mother."

Some of Betty's schoolmates at the convent school thought of her as Spanish, an identification she eagerly accepted. She surprised the nuns by making an address to the student body in Spanish; and for the first time she began to call herself Lola. The name was a diminutive form of her second Christian name, Dolores. Never, from the time of her birth, had anyone addressed her or referred to her as Maria, and henceforth she would use "Lola" more and more frequently, until "Betty," which she still associated with her mother, was dropped entirely.

When Sir Jasper and Lady Nicolls returned to London with their charges in 1832, the fourteen-year-old Betty was surprised to learn that her mother was taking a new interest in her. Sometime within the next year, Mrs. Craigie wrote her daughter, she would make her first visit to England in a decade and would take the girl back to India with her.

If Mrs. Craigie thought Betty would be delighted, she was badly mistaken. From the outset she insisted that her mother must have an undeclared reason for wanting to take her to India and implored Lady Nicolls to help her find out what it was. Unaware of Betty's hostility to her mother, which Betty had been careful to conceal, Lady Nicolls became her accomplice and wrote Mrs. Craigie a long letter.

Mail took four to five months each way, so Mrs. Craigie's reply did not reach England until 1833, shortly before the lady herself arrived. The letter wasted no words: As Lady Nicolls well knew, Mrs. Craigie wrote, attractive wives were at a premium in India, and she had arranged a brilliant marriage for her daughter. Betty would be married upon her arrival in India to Sir Abraham Lumley, a wealthy barrister who held a seat as Lord Justice on the Royal Indian Supreme Court. Betty Gilbert would become Lady Lumley.

The future Lady Lumley was immediately suspicious. Why, she wondered, would a man in Sir Abraham's position be willing to marry an untitled stranger? She learned the truth from Fanny Nicolls, Sir Jasper's youngest daughter and her close friend and confidante.

Sir Abraham, Betty was told, was a sixty-year-old widower who suffered from gout. In addition, he was short, plump, and exceptionally homely. He tried to compensate for his physical shortcomings by leading an active life as a ladies' man, and his many flirtations were the joke of the viceregal court.

To a girl who had just turned fifteen the idea of marriage to a man of Sir Abraham's age was a nightmare. He must be on the verge of senility, she told Fanny. Under no circumstances would she be cajoled, persuaded, fooled, or forced into becoming Lady Lumley. She had no idea how she would circumvent her mother's plan, but she swore a dramatic oath that she would escape from the net about to be dropped over her.

The seeming anticlimax that followed these revelations was a letdown. There was no further word from India. Perhaps, for reasons beyond Betty's knowledge, the scheme had been abandoned.

Sir Jasper, for one, had never taken it seriously, and late in the summer of 1833, he sent Betty and Fanny, appropriately chaperoned, to Bath, the watering resort most favored by fashionable English society. There the girls would live for six months at least. They would polish their deportment, observe the conduct of their elders, and prepare to take their own places in society when they returned to London by early spring.

What Betty and her guardians did not know was that Mrs. Craigie had already sailed from India for England, to bring Sir Abraham's bride back to India. Maria Dolores Gilbert was spending her last months as an innocent in the world of adults.

[CHAPTER II]

The reunion of Mrs. Craigie and her daughter after a separation of seven years was pleasant and courteous, with both principals concealing their hostilities. Mrs. Craigie was able to confirm the reports that her daughter had become a beautiful woman, and Betty—according to her later, candid admission in her *Autobiography*—saw that her mother was still exceptionally handsome, although somewhat less so than she was in Betty's memory. Relieved to discover that her mother was no rival, she behaved more cordially than she might have.

The visit proved to be far more pleasant than Betty had imagined. Her mother was prepared to spend a large sum of money on a new wardrobe for her, and Betty, who had been clothed only by her various temporary benefactors through the years, was delighted. Bath was filled with England's most exclusive dressmakers and milliners, cobblers and glovers, and Mrs. Craigie seemed determined to visit all of them. Betty spent hours each day enduring the exquisite torture of fittings, then accompanied her mother on another round of visits to shops. Mrs. Craigie bought her more gowns, shoes, hats, and lingerie at one time than she had owned in her whole life and Betty, assuming that her mother was making up for years of neglect, happily thanked her for each piece of finery.

There were other excitements, notably the continuing presence of her mother's escort, First Lieutenant Thomas James of the 21st

Regiment of Native Infantry (Bengal), who had been Mrs. Craigie's shipmate on the long voyage from India. Lieutenant James had taken advantage of the happenstance to attach himself to the wife of a powerful senior officer, who could be helpful in advancing his career. In his plumed helmet, scarlet tunic, tight-fitting white breeches, and cavalry boots, the twenty-seven-year-old James was easily the most dashing man the impressionable young girl had ever met.

Lieutenant James acted as errand boy without complaint, and at luncheon and dinner he happily escorted Mrs. Craigie and Betty to Bath's most fashionable inns and restaurants. A more observant woman might have noticed that the young officer was strongly attracted to his patroness' lovely daughter, but Mrs. Craigie was preoccupied with her own scheme.

Not until she had spent two weeks at Bath did Mrs. Craigie tell her daughter that she must return to India and marry Sir Abraham Lumley. Betty protested loudly, but neither tears nor rages had any effect on her mother, who believed she had arranged a perfect union.

When Betty found she could not sway her mother, she turned to Fanny Nicolls, who could offer her nothing but sympathy. That left Lieutenant James, with whom she was infatuated and who was fascinated by her.

Whether an elopement was her idea or his, or grew naturally out of Betty's desire to escape from an impossible predicament, is difficult to determine—but it should have surprised no one.

Literally no details of the elopement have survived. James was not a man who put pen to paper unless he was writing an official military report, and the usually verbose Lola says nothing in her autobiography or elsewhere about the matter. The facts obtainable from other sources can be summarized very briefly: after an interlude of six weeks, the couple appeared in County Meath, Ireland, where James's family lived, and Betty was placed under the protection of his relatives. At this point Lola resumes the story of her life, declaring that she and James had great difficulty in trying to get married since she was not yet of age and needed parental consent.

Understandably reluctant to face Mrs. Craigie, James sent his unmarried sister to negotiate on his behalf. Miss James found the lady still residing in Bath, reasoning that sooner or later Betty and the lieutenant would make an attempt to get in touch with her there. The meetings of the two women could not have been pleasant, but Mrs. Craigie finally became convinced that under no circumstances would her daughter return to become the wife of Sir Abraham Lumley. Common sense dictated the need for an immediate marriage: Betty would be regarded as a fallen woman if she remained single after her elopement.

Mrs. Craigie finally gave her written consent to the marriage, but refused to attend the wedding and made it clear that the young couple did not have her blessing. For all practical purposes that ended her active involvement in her daughter's life. Their paths would cross again, briefly, in India, but the new break was too serious to mend and, on the few occasions when they saw each other, they confined themselves to civilities.

Lola's comments on her marriage to James, which took place in County Meath on July 23, 1834, have all the perception of hindsight. In her autobiography she writes:

> So, in flying from that marriage with ghastly and gouty old age, the child lost her mother, and gained what proved to be only the outside shell of a husband, who had neither a brain she could respect, nor a heart which it was possible for her to love. He reminded her of a toy soldier, its head filled with sawdust, a creature that could be manipulated at will, and lacked a mind and will of its own.
>
> Runaway matches, like runaway horses, are almost sure to end in a smash-up. My advice to all young girls who contemplate taking such a step is that they had better hang or drown themselves just one hour before they start.

Her disillusionment, however, was not immediate. A number of parties were given for the newlyweds, and Lieutenant James took his bride to Dublin, where she was presented to the Lord Lieutenant, Lord Normanby. The colony of English rulers in the Irish capital welcomed the couple, and the bachelor officers of the garrison were particularly attentive to the radiant bride. In view of Lola's later activities, it is probable that the bride engaged in a number of flirtations during her sojourn in Dublin. By now it was impossible for her to meet any man without trying to subjugate him, so there may have been good cause for the jealousy she ascribes to her husband in her autobiography.

Lieutenant James was not a man to remain idle while his bride smiled at other men. He took her off for a hunting and fishing trip on the west coast of Ireland, where for days at a time they spoke to no outsider except an occasional farmer. Betty, who hated isolation even more than she hated outdoor sports or camping in the open, was miserable.

The ordeal did not end until the late autumn of 1834, when Lieutenant James's furlough came to an end and he had to rejoin his regiment. He traveled to London with his wife, the extensive wardrobe her mother had supplied filling many leather boxes, and together they sailed for the East on a large merchantman, the *Blunt*.

The parallels between the mother's and daughter's course are so obvious that the new Mrs. James must have been aware of them. Like her mother, Betty had married an impoverished young officer who had no fortune of his own and no friends in high places to promote his career. Like her mother, she was setting out to make a new life for herself in India. But there were significant differences: Maria Dolores James may have been no more eager than her mother to win the favor of every man she met, but her motivation for doing so was far more intense. Her own life had been so lonely and insecure that at sixteen she was already certain she could depend only on herself if she hoped to better her lot.

The voyage to India was uneventful, even if one believes the account of it in Lola's autobiography. Lieutenant James, she writes, imbibed so freely of gin, rum, and porter on the trip that he was seldom sober. In fact, she claims, he drank himself into insensibility on most days. His personnel record, still on file at the War Office, gives no indication that he found alcohol a problem; Lola may have made up the story to win the sympathy of her readers. In her later years, with her reputation as a femme fatale at stake, she apparently felt it necessary to titillate her audience, or, at the very least, to establish her credentials as a beauty whom all men found irresistible. Whatever her motives, she devotes a small section of her autobiography to the voyage, claiming that three "harmless flirtations" helped her escape the boredom of spending all her days and evenings with an intoxicated husband.

All three of her swains, she says, were in the habit of slipping notes under her cabin door. With some amusement she describes using these notes later in the evening as spills to light her husband's pipe, not explaining how a man so drunk he couldn't stay conscious managed to smoke a pipe.

One of her admirers, according to Lola, was a Spaniard named Enríquez, and another was an Englishman named John. She offers her readers no details about either. The third was no less than the captain of the ship, whom she describes as a "colossal sailor, a giant of a man with a full beard, eyes as bright as they were wise, and surrounded by an air of masculine self-esteem." The captain was something of a philosopher as well, if Lola's tale is to be believed. She quotes a number of his profound observations on the human condition, one example of which should suffice: "Love is a pipe we fill at eighteen, and smoke till forty; then we rake the ashes till our exit."

We can assume that in one way or another Mrs. James escaped the tedium of the long voyage. Whatever was happening to the marriage, the bride was looking forward to her return to India. She had known her happiest childhood years there and, thanks to her relationship with nurses and orderlies, had a greater understanding of India and its people than most Englishmen, who led isolated garrison lives. She had seen little of the poverty, famine, and cruelty that were the predominant characteristics of life in the East, and had spent no time in the native towns and villages. But she had a ready grasp of the Indian mind, sympathized with it, and to a surprising degree could identify herself with it. An absence from India of nearly a decade had cost her some of her command of classical Hindi and various dialects, but she quickly regained her proficiency.

In Calcutta the Jameses were given temporary quarters at Fort William. For a time it amused Betty to pretend that she knew none of the Indian tongues, which enabled her to listen to the conversation of servants without their realizing it. But when she heard them describe her in flattering terms, she could not resist talking with them in their own languages, which further enhanced her popularity in native circles.

Lieutenant James spent the better part of a year in Calcutta, where his wife—who referred to herself as Lola with increasing frequency—repeated her mother's success of a generation earlier. According to descriptions of Mrs. James in letters written by the Hon. Emily Eden, the sister of Lord Auckland, the new viceroy, Lola was exceptionally pretty. Five feet, eight inches, she was unusually tall, with thick auburn hair that fell to her waist, a superb figure, and blue eyes "of remarkable clarity."

Within a short time she was the belle of the viceregal court. Her dance card was filled days before a ball, and she was surrounded by officers and civil servants at teas, receptions, and levees. She enjoyed a daily canter, on which she might be accompanied by as many as a dozen officers. It became impossible for her to attend to her own errands; "platoons" of officers acted as her escorts wherever she went shopping.

If Lieutenant James had been jealous of the attentions paid his wife by fellow officers in Dublin, he had far greater cause now. But Betty either cared so little for him by now or was so pleasantly occupied that her husband's reaction failed to inspire so much as a paragraph in her autobiography. Her ego was feasting. The disintegration of the marriage could hardly have been the exclusive fault of Lieutenant James, but his emotionally immature wife, not yet eighteen, accepted no share of the blame.

In the winter of 1836, Betty's Calcutta idyll came to an end. Lieutenant James was transferred to a lonely military garrison at Karnal, a town located about halfway between Delhi and Simla, on the ancient Jumna Canal. The social life there was far simpler than at the court of the viceroy; the influence of the Anglican clergy was strong at these interior posts, and the chaplain was almost as influential as the brigadier or colonel in command. Any British wife living at a small Indian station located far from direct contact with Western civilization knew that married couples were expected to conduct themselves in accordance with the proprieties. Mrs. James acompanied her husband to Karnal with the greatest reluctance.

Neither Lola nor her contemporaries realized it in the winter of 1836, but a new era had already begun. The moral influence of young Princess Victoria was already making itself felt throughout the Empire, and although she had not yet succeeded her uncle, the ailing King William IV, to the throne, her standards were being accepted everywhere as a model. More than ever, young officers' wives were expected to behave.

Betty had acted the part of a chameleon through so much of her childhood that she found the change in role from flirtatious belle to decorous officer's wife easy enough to manage. The wives of senior officers spoke of her with admiration, which was always the acid test.

Early in 1838 Betty's life was further complicated and restricted when the field command of the Indian Army was transferred to the garrison city of Simla. Among those who moved there were Brigadier John Craigie, now deputy adjutant general of the entire force, and his wife.

Betty had not seen her mother since the elopement from Bath, but a meeting was unavoidable when, in the late spring of 1838, Lieutenant James was required to visit Simla on official business. In accordance with protocol, his wife accompanied him.

Lieutenant James, acutely aware of the power wielded by his wife's stepfather, made it his business to make amends to Mrs. Craigie. His success in charming her is verified by the correspondence of Miss Eden, who visited Simla the following January, at which time the officers stationed at outlying garrisons came to the city with their wives to pay their respects to her. When Brigadier and Mrs. Craigie called, they were accompanied by Lieutenant and Mrs. James, and Miss Eden, who knew their story, took a sharp-eyed interest in the relationships. Betty James, to whom Miss Eden referred in her letters as "charming and very pretty," was on good terms with her stepfather, and they were "much at ease together." The same could not be said of Mrs. Craigie and her daughter. The mother, obviously nervous, tried to hide her irritation whenever Miss Eden addressed her daughter, who went through all the motions of treating Mrs. Craigie with polite respect.

Lieutenant James, however, more than made up for his wife's coolness; his devotion to his mother-in-law was evident. According to Miss Eden he was "a smart looking man, with bright waistcoats and bright teeth, with a showy horse, and he was unflagging in his attentions to *ma belle mère*. His motives were patently transparent, but I must admit the show he staged was an imposing sight, and I cannot see any way out of it but magnanimous admiration."

The Jameses remained in Simla for several weeks in order to attend various functions given in honor of the Viceroy's sister, and in her letters Miss Eden frequently commented on Betty's appearance and character. "Mrs. James," she wrote on the morning after a dinner party, "is undoubtedly the prettiest girl in India, and is such a merry, unaffected person. She is so youthful that one thinks of her as a child of no more than fourteen or fifteen. When one ponders on the fact that she and her husband will pass their entire lives in India, one does not wonder at Mrs. Craigie's resentment at her having run away to be married."

At the end of a month's stay in Simla, during which time Lord Auckland joined her, Miss Eden wrote that Betty and her stepfather had achieved a complete reconciliation. The relations of mother and daughter remained strained, however, with each apparently unwilling or unable to trust the other.

The viceregal visit concluded, Cinderella went back to her straitlaced garrison life to spend long days dreaming under the blazing Indian sun. The months passed slowly. In November of 1839, when Miss Eden had returned to India after an extended tour of the Orient, she and her party paid a visit to the garrison at Karnal:

That pretty Mrs. James looked like a star among the others. I do not wonder that when a tolerable-looking girl comes up into this remote country she is persecuted with proposals, most of them dishonorable.

At the end of the brief visit, she wrote:

We left Karnal yesterday morning. Little Mrs. James was so unhappy at our going that we asked her to come and pass the day with us in the field on our travels. She went from tent to tent, and chattered all the day, and visited her friend, Mrs.——, who is with the camp. I gave her a pink silk gown, and it was altogether a very happy day for her. It ended in her going back to Karnal on my elephant, with E. N. by her side and Lieutenant James sitting behind. She had never been on an elephant before, and thought it delightful.

She is very pretty, and a good little thing, apparently, but they are very poor, and she is very young and lively. If she falls into bad hands she would soon laugh herself into foolish scrapes. At present the husband and wife are very fond of each other, but a girl who marries at fifteen hardly knows what she likes."

Whether the Jameses were "very fond of each other" at this time or were putting up a front for the benefit of the Viceroy's sister is not easy to determine, but it is reasonable to assume the latter: within months of Miss Eden's departure, the marriage fell apart. The direct cause, according to Lola, was a Mrs. Lomer, the wife of the civilian administrator of Karnal.

The James and Lomer families were neighbors in the garrison compound. Each morning before reporting for duty, Lieutenant James, whose promotion to a captaincy became effective in the midst of his domestic crisis, went off with Mrs. Lomer for an early morning canter. One morning, Lola states in her autobiography, they failed to return, and it eventually developed that they had run off to the Neilghery Hills.

This story is highly questionable. Lieutenant James would have been forced to resign his commission at the very least; and having been absent without leave, it is probable that he would have been court-martialed. It should be noted, too, that the Neilghery Hills lay a long 1,436 miles from Karnal, much of the territory in regions where the dominion of the British raj had not yet been established. It is beyond credulity that Captain James would have made such a journey alone, much less accompanied by the wife of a civilian colleague.

Whatever the actual cause of the marital break, Betty left her husband and went to Calcutta, where she found temporary refuge under the roof of her mother and stepfather, now Major General John Craigie. Betty received her customary warm welcome from Craigie, but her mother was even chillier than usual. One reason, perhaps, was the timing of the visit: it was rumored that General Craigie would soon be awarded a knighthood, and his wife may have feared a family scandal, which would hurt his chances for the honor.

Mrs. Craigie announced that the heat of Karnal had been injurious to Betty's health, so she was being sent to the colder climate of England to recuperate. Arrangements were made for her to sail on a packet ship, and in January, 1841, Betty boarded the *Larkin.*

Her mother did not see her off, but General Craigie escorted Betty to the ship. According to the accounts of several witnesses, he and his stepdaughter both wept as he kissed her goodby. He also gave Betty the sum of £1000 and urged her to buy a house for herself in the country outside London.

A few moments before the ship weighed anchor, Captain James appeared at the dock. Presumably Betty had not known he was in Calcutta, and nobody knew why he decided to see his wife leave India. One thing is certain, the farewells on both side were frosty. The separate correspondence of two witnesses indicates that the young wife stood rigidly on the deck during the brief moments she and her husband of seven years confronted each other. Then, with great reluctance, she extended her hand to him.

As nearly as can be determined, neither Betty nor Captain James made any plans for a divorce. This circumstance alone casts doubt on Lola's claim that Captain James ran away with Mrs. Lomer. English law permitted divorce only on the grounds of adultery, and had James given his wife this opportunity, she would have been foolish to reject it. There is also no record of any action having been taken by the cuckolded Mr. Lomer, who, as a civilian employee of Queen Victoria's government, would surely have preserved his own reputation by filing a divorce suit of his own.

The inescapable conclusion is that, like so many other stories told by Lola Montez in her autobiography and in newspaper interviews, the James-Lomer affair was invented out of whole cloth.

Captain James had his wife placed under surveillance after her return to England, a great financial burden for an officer who lacked private means. But he seemed convinced that his detectives would obtain the evidence he needed to file a suit, which suggests that his wife's conduct may not have been above reproach during her last year at Karnal.

Whatever the circumstances may have been, the break between Captain James and his wife was irrevocable. Betty—Lola—was alone in the world at the age of twenty-two.

[CHAPTER III]

The man who squired Betty James down the path that led to her notoriety as Lola Montez was named Lennox. That much can be established, but almost nothing more is known about him, despite his seeming importance in her life.

Lennox was one of the passengers on board the *Larkin* when the packet ship sailed for England. Presumably he did not board the ship at Calcutta, but was already a passenger when the vessel put in there. He was subsequently called Captain Lennox in Captain James's divorce suit and, according to a brief letter sent to General Craigie by his brother David, was aide-de-camp to the British governor of some distant colony. There are no records of an officer named Lennox who was active in either the Royal Navy or Army at that time, however, so it is useless to speculate further on his identity. It must suffice that he is the first genuine villain in Lola's story.

When Betty first boarded the packet ship, her stepfather put her in the care of an elderly American couple from Boston, a Mr. and Mrs. Sturges, who seemed willing enough to accept the charge. Or so Craigie wrote his brother in Perth, Scotland, asking him to meet the ship and take the girl home with him until she recovered her equilibrium.

Young Mrs. James, however, had other plans.

Whether Betty was genuinely charmed by Lennox or whether she just happened to have a use for him, no one knows. It may be true, as she claims in her autobiography, that he seduced her; but it is equally possible, considering her desire to make every man her slave, that she pursued him. Regardless of who did the chasing, Lennox and Betty had four months on board ship in which to get acquainted, and by the time the *Larkin* sailed up the Thames to London, they were lovers.

David Craigie was waiting at the docks to take his brother's stepdaughter with him back to Perth, but Betty chose this moment in her life to proclaim her independence. She would be twenty-three in a few weeks, she knew she was beautiful, and the gloomy mists of the north held no appeal for her. Mr. Craigie tried his best to persuade her to come with him, but was forced to admit defeat and went off alone after writing his brother a sad letter.

London was the largest metropolis in the Western world, the capital of a growing empire, the site of fifty theaters and innumerable shops, inns, taverns, and restaurants. Betty James reveled in the luxury of her new freedom. The center of attention wherever she went, she did not object too strenuously when men followed her through the streets. She regarded any form of admiration as a tribute to her beauty.

She also pursued her affair with Lennox. Immediately after her arrival, she took up quarters at the Imperial Hotel, and after a stay of several weeks there found a small apartment in St. James's. Lennox visited her frequently, and whenever he came to her, he remained for the night.

Betty accepted no money from him. She was proud of her independence, and thought herself fortunate to be able to maintain it. In addition to the £1000 General Craigie had given her as she left India, she had some jewelry and a little money she had managed to save. In all, according to her autobiography, her total nest egg amounted to some $10,000. That amount may be an exaggeration, but Betty James must have had a fair amount of money for the 1840's.

By her own admission she frittered her little fortune away over the next year and a half, her only excuse being that she had suffered from "an insensible perspiration, which is a disease very common to the purses of ladies who have never been taught the value of money." Her flat was expensive, she bought any new clothes that caught her eye, and she rode about town in a rented carriage. For eighteen months she lived the grand life—until late in 1842, when she suddenly faced a crisis.

Just as her funds were nearly exhausted, Captain James filed suit for divorce in the Consistory Court of London. He charged her with misconduct, naming Lennox as co-respondent. Attached to his petition were affidavits sworn by his private detectives, stipulating specific occasions—both at the Imperial Hotel in Covent Garden and at Betty's flat in St. James's—on which she had slept with Lennox. Since she was guilty, and perhaps indifferent, she did not contest the suit.

The court granted Captain James a divorce *a mensa et toro.* In effect this was a legal separation: each of the principals was directed not to remarry during the lifetime of the other. This meant that should either elect to do so, the new union would not be recognized as legal in Great Britain or any portion of the empire. It was a ruling that Lola Montez would flout repeatedly.

Lennox promptly disappeared from Betty's life. If his mistress was disturbed by his failure to help her in a time of stress, she never indicated it to anyone.

Captain James, too, dropped out of his former wife's life. He remained in the Indian Army until 1856, when he retired with the rank of lieutenant colonel; returning to England shortly thereafter, he lived in retirement until 1871. One marriage had been enough for him, and he made no more trips to the altar. He maintained a dignified silence on the subject of Lola Montez after she achieved international notoriety, consistently refusing to discuss her with newsmen. When her death was reported to him on the eve of the American Civil War, he told reporters, "I'm sorry to hear it," but would make no additional comment.

Betty—twenty-four years old, divorced, lacking friends or patrons, and all but destitute—faced a precarious future.

London was a city of bewildering contradictions. The Industrial Revolution was in full swing, new factories were springing up everywhere, and the nation was growing rich and powerful. The wealthy were becoming still wealthier, and the expanding middle class lived better than ever before, but the poverty of the working class was appalling. It was customary for men to work sixteen hours a day or longer in the new industrial plants, and illiterate women and children suffered the same fate.

The cruelty of the age was almost beyond belief. Public executions of criminals became circuses that made the poor forget their hunger for the moment—and served a warning that the same fate awaited those who dared to defy the law. The upper classes showed no respect for that same law, and gangs of young gentlemen amused themselves by searching the streets for a policeman, beating him senseless, and then pouring green paint over him. Bearfighting and cockfighting were among the sports that drew the largest crowds, and the blood lust of all classes seemed never to be satiated. At least twenty murders were committed each day in London. Armed robberies and mayhem were common, and the poor drank gin to help them forget their plight. Prostitution was rampant, and although accurate statistics are hard to obtain, some of the best qualified contemporary observers, including an indignant minority of members of Parliament, estimated that there were at least 25,000 poor women of all ages selling themselves in the streets.

The former Mrs. James had no intention of suffocating in the quicksands of London. Snubbed by reputable society after her divorce, she had to act quickly. Only one career was open to a woman in the 1840's—the stage—so Betty made up her mind to become an actress.

London's best-known dramatic coach was a former actress

named Fanny Kelly, who had worked wonders with several prominent actresses. For three months of lessons Betty paid Miss Kelly a substantial portion of her dwindling financial reserves. Miss Kelly worked hard with her, but could do little with the self-admiring young girl who had no experience and no discernible talent.

Recognizing her own limitations, Betty decided to attack from a different direction. If she could not be a new Sarah Siddons, she would win success as a dancer. Planning her campaign like a general preparing a siege, she went off to Madrid to take dancing lessons from a renowned teacher named Hernandez.

How Betty financed the journey and managed to live for several months in Madrid—much less pay for her lessons—is something of a mystery. She makes no mention of this period of her life in her autobiography and, when questioned about it by reporters years later, gave evasive answers. It is reasonable to assume that she acquired funds for her project by selling her rather spectacular personal charms to one or more gentlemen willing to pay a high price for them. She still owned her expensive wardrobe, she still spoke and acted like a lady, so there was nothing to prevent her from frequenting the dining rooms of the prominent hotels that catered to wealthy foreign visitors. The rest would have been easy for an expert flirt.

However she acquired the money, Betty went to Madrid with a full purse and lived accordingly, taking quarters in a fashionable section of the city and plunging into her dancing lessons. But dancing was only a portion of what she learned in the Spanish capital. Betty James had decided to acquire a completely new name and identity, partly because she wanted no additional unfavorable publicity in the wake of Captain James's divorce action against her, and partly because she had learned that London theatrical managers paid their highest wages to prominent foreign singers, dancers, and actresses. And so Betty studied the people around her, spending hours each day under the awnings of the cafes that were becoming increasingly popular in the major Spanish cities.

Unfortunately the only women who went alone to these places

were anything but ladies—young ladies always being accompanied by their duennas when they left their homes. The women Betty studied were harlots, and the mannerisms she acquired were those of the higher-priced strumpets. It is small wonder that in her Spanish role Lola Montez would remind those who had traveled extensively of Madrid's more expensive prostitutes. It can also be argued that she had a natural predilection for such a part, and documentary evidence supports the theory.

Betty returned to London in late spring, using the name of Lola Montez and speaking with a faint but distinct Spanish accent. Her beauty, as well as her slight air of foreign mystery, gained her admittance to the offices of theatrical managers, and within a few days she made her first deal to appear on the stage.

An advertisement appeared in the newspapers to the effect that on Saturday, June 3, 1843, at the Theatre Royal, a special treat awaited patrons attending *The Barber of Seville.* Donna Lola Montez, the prima ballerina of the Teatro Real, Seville, making her first appearance in Great Britain, would perform the original Spanish dance *El Olano.*

The theater critic who wrote for the *Telegraph* under the initial "Q" was struck by the advertisement and, hoping to gain a head start on his colleagues, requested permission to attend a rehearsal. Lola was delighted, and she took the precaution of chatting with him for some time in the auditorium of the theater before she went up onto the stage. She believed that if she succeeded in charming him, he would be inclined to overlook any flaws in her performance—she was still too much the realist to entertain any illusions about her talents.

Q's article, which was printed in the *Telegraph* of Thursday, June 1, was all Lola could have wanted:

> Her figure was even more attractive than her face, lovely as the latter was. Lithe and graceful as a young fawn, every movement that she made seemed filled with melody as she commenced her dance. Her eyes were blazing and flashing with excitement, for she felt that I was prepared to admire her. In her pose, grace seemed

involuntarily to preside over her limbs and dispose their attitude. Her foot and ankle were almost faultless.

Nadaud, the violinist, drew his bow across his instrument, and she began to dance. No one will quarrel with me for saying that she is not a finished danseuse, but all will as certainly agree with me that she possesses every element which could be required, with careful study, to make her eminent in her vocation. As she swept round the stage, her slender waist swayed to the music, and her graceful head and neck bent with it, like a flower that bends with the impulse given to its stem by the changing and fitful temper of the wind.

Thanks to Q's generous praise, Lola and the manager of the Theatre Royal anticipated a great success. The royal box was filled on the night of the performance, with the Queen Dowager and her brother-in-law the King of Hanover in attendance. Also present in the theater were the Duchess of Kent and the Duke and Duchess of Cambridge.

At the conclusion of the first act of the opera, the lights were lowered and the curtains opened to reveal the interior of a Moorish hall. A maidservant stood upstage, waiting for someone, and suddenly Lola Montez appeared, swathed in a voluminous Spanish shawl. She handed one end of the material to the maid, then twirled across the stage, releasing herself from the garment. Monday's *Herald* offered its readers a rhapsodic word portrait of the young woman who was attempting to pass herself off before her fellow Englishmen as a talented member of the Spanish nobility:

What a lovely picture she is to contemplate! There is before you the perfection of Spanish beauty—the tall, handsome person, the full, lustrous eye, the joyous, animated face and the intensely auburn hair of the Spanish aristocracy. She is dressed, too, in the brightest of colors: the petticoat is dappled with flaunting hints of red, yellow and violet, and its showy diversities of hue are enforced by the black velvet bodice above, which confines the bust with an unscrupulous pinch. Presently this Andalusian Papagena lifts her arms, and the sharp, merry crack of the castanets is heard. She has commenced one of the lovely dances of her people, and many a piquant grace does she unfold . . .

The audience, according to the less ecstatic *Times*, seemed to be bewitched, and before the dance had ended, bouquets of flowers were thrown onto the stage as tribute to the new rage of London. The dancer sank to the floor at the end of her number in a deep curtsy to the wildly applauding audience.

Then, as the applause died away, a male voice boomed from one of the boxes: "Lola Montez?" its owner demanded. "She's Betty James, that's who she is!"

The gallery began to hiss, other patrons joined in, and eventually the near-rage of London was forced to flee into the wings, her debut ruined.

Obviously the heckler was someone who had known her in her previous identity, but the more responsible newspapers, which printed a factual account of the debacle, did not name him. Many years later Lola herself was the authority for the assertion that he was her enemy, Lord Ranelagh, and that he became her foe because she had rebuffed his advances. She did not explain why she had waited so long before bringing his name into the open, but the story is a good one, and if it happened to be less than truthful, it succeeded in transforming a laughingstock into a heroine.

Lola fought back against her accuser, and in an impassioned letter to the *Era* defended herself by creating a number of straw men, which she then demolished. Reports were being circulated about her by foes unknown, she declared, the most vicious of them being a canard that claimed she had long been one of London's more disreputable characters. She was a native of Seville, and was paying the first visit of her life to London, a city she found less than pleasant because it was inhabited by so many members of the gentry who were not true gentlemen.

Her lawyer, she said, had been instructed to file suit for slander against her persecutors, and she was certain to emerge triumphant. Affidavits from lifelong friends and business associates in Seville would prove that place was her home. She further called attention to the fact that she had arrived in London by ship from Spain, setting foot on English soil early on the morning of May 14. The records of the immigration authorities proclaimed her innocence to the entire world.

The letter, however magnificent a bluff, failed to procure Lola another engagement. Theatrical managers were leery of her and, having no desire to invite ridicule, refused to hire her. For all practical purposes she could obtain no employment in the London theater.

It might have been possible for her to arrange dancing appearances in the provinces, but her memories of small-town Scotland were still vivid, and she knew that at best she would be regarded as something of a freak. Her ambition had been fired by her near-success, along with a fierce desire to win financial independence that would make her obligated to no one for the rest of her life.

The Continent beckoned, and when her letter to the *Era* failed to produce the results she sought, Lola packed all of her belongings and on June 15, 1843, set sail for Ostende. She had just enough money in her purse to pay for a one-way ticket to Brussels, which necessarily became her immediate destination.

[CHAPTER IV]

A woman named Clara Magruder, a neighbor of Lola Montez' in rural California in the mid-1850's, interviewed her at length about her earlier life for a magazine article, which appeared in *Harper's Weekly*. Miss Magruder wrote:

> Lola and I talked frankly about many things on our walks and rides together through the hills. What bothered her most was being called a w—— by people who believed all the lies that were written about her. She told me that she never earned her living as a prostitute except for one short period, and she wasn't ashamed to admit it. She ran off to Brussels at the very beginning of her career because so many people in England were being mean to her, and she didn't have a red cent to her name. So she did what any other woman would have done in the same position, and she earned her living in the only way she could. That doesn't make her bad!

Lola's purse was empty when she reached Brussels on June 17, 1843, beginning ten months of wandering that would take her to Berlin, Dresden, Warsaw, and St. Petersburg. Her depleted financial state did not prevent her from taking lodgings at a small, exclusive hotel located only a stone's throw from the Hotel Grand Place. Nor did it stop her from visiting the hotel's dining room on her first evening there to order a full-course dinner.

Supremely conscious of her precarious state, she must have

planned her moves with care. There were only a few theaters in still provincial Brussels, none of which wanted to employ an unknown dancer who said she came from Spain. Lola knew that she needed considerable sums to maintain the façade of a lady and that her only assets of the moment were her extraordinary beauty of face and figure. Men turned to stare at her on the boulevards, but she knew her descent into the gutter would be swift if she gave in to the temptation to become a streetwalker. If she was to build a nest egg sufficiently large to allow her to pursue her career as a dancer, she would have to exercise discretion.

As she had discovered before making her journey to Madrid, a hotel dining room was a perfect place for a young lady to arrange a temporary liaison with a businessman who was a stranger to the city. On three nights in a row, she later told Mrs. Magruder, she earned enough to give herself a breathing spell. At least she had money in her purse now to pay for a two-week stay at the hotel and to take care of her meals and sundries.

A far different story is told by A. D. Vandam in *An Englishman in Paris,* published in London in 1892. Lola was so extravagant in some of her claims that she sometimes sparked the imagination of enthusiastic biographers. Vandam cites no sources, so it is hard to determine whether he invented his version or had access to factual material unearthed by other writers.

In any event, Vandam wrote, Lola did not sell herself to businessmen visiting Brussels; she was reduced to singing in the streets as she begged for coppers. Inasmuch as Lola was booed off the stage on the few occasions when she tried to sing, and could not by her own admission carry a tune, it seems unlikely that passersby would throw her enough coins to pay for her room and board at one of the most exclusive hotels in Brussels. Common sense suggests that Mrs. Magruder's is the more reliable account.

One of Lola's customers during her brief stay in Brussels was a prominent Prussian whose identity remains clouded. In several interviews given many years later, Lola hinted that he was a high-ranking diplomat, but this claim may have been a feeble attempt to add glamour to an otherwise sordid incident. Earlier stories called him a wealthy businessman. He was traveling in his own coach, and when he offered to take Lola away with him, she leaped at the opportunity.

There are some discrepancies regarding the itinerary of Lola and her German benefactor, whoever he may have been. According to some accounts, he took her with him to Russian-occupied Poland and used his influence there to help her obtain a position with the Opera as a dancer. Other stories, including Lola's, have it that he escorted her to Berlin. Regardless of how she got there, Lola did go to Berlin.

The basic character of a city, like that of a person, undergoes few changes over the years; even as far back as the early 1840's, Berlin was known as the crudest, least sophisticated of European capitals. The Junkers, an ancient class of wealthy landowners, were the power behind the throne as they had been for centuries. They lived in a tightly knit society virtually closed to all outsiders, including beautiful, foreign would-be dancers who were reduced to living as adventuresses. Since Frederick the Great created the finest army in Europe a century earlier, the martial spirit had pervaded every level of Berlin's life. The Prussian regiments had given a good account of themselves in the Napoleonic Wars, and only the English were reluctant to credit them with the decisive role in Napoleon's defeat at Waterloo.

Family life was of paramount importance to the Prussians, who were determined to extend their influence into other German-speaking nations and principalities. But they were realists nonetheless: an expensive brothel district had been created where high-ranking officers, who gave lip service to the strict moral standards of the nation, could lay those standards aside in private moments.

Certainly it was unthinkable that any woman other than a lady of impeccable virtue would be granted admittance to the royal court. Yet Lola Montez asserted over many years that she had had a brief but impassioned love affair with King Frederick

William IV. Contemporaries who knew Prussia, particularly those who knew the monarch, openly ridiculed her for this claim. Like his father before him, Frederick William was a narrow-minded conservative and, in his personal life, home-loving and circumspect. His views were so orthodox, in fact, that for many years he refused to permit the mention of Frederick the Great's name in his presence—because his illustrious predecessor had been homosexual.

Had the king succumbed to Lola's charms, he would never have indulged in an affair with her at his palace outside Berlin, where his court and the entire diplomatic corps would have learned of it. And since he lived nowhere else in the summer and autumn of 1843, he could have enjoyed a liaison with Lola only at his own palace or its environs.

The diplomats accredited to the court of Frederick William IV during the period make no mention in their correspondence of any such affair. The ministers and other officials of Prussia were silent, too, and not even the satiric poets of Berlin, who found an escape from moral tyranny by writing impudent lyrics, scribbled a single word on the subject.

Lola is the sole, highly dubious authority for the claim that her Prussian benefactor took her to court and introduced her to the king, who immediately made himself her willing slave. In later years, when she wore the decorations given her by Ludwig of Bavaria, she often sported a small gold Prussian cross, too—"a gift of Frederick William." No one has ever found out where she actually acquired it.

However she passed the time there, Lola left Berlin two or three weeks later for Warsaw; possibly accompanied by her Prussian benefactor, possibly traveling alone.

The wealthy nobles of Poland, and the artists, writers, and composers who lived at their miniature courts, called Warsaw the "Paris of the East," but the name was as exaggerated as one of Lola's stories. Of all Europe's great cities, Warsaw was the most miserable. Life there had been barely tolerable since Russian legions, with the connivance of Prussia, had savagely crushed the revolt that had broken out in 1830. Vigorous attempts were being made by the Russians to eliminate Polish culture, traditions and patriotic sentiment. The University of Warsaw had been closed for a decade, and the most promising students, if they had the funds, were required to attend school either in St. Petersburg or Kiev. Pressures were exerted on the Roman Catholic Church to prevent the Polish bishops and priests from making patriotic remarks in the pulpit. Theaters and other places of entertainment were subjected to severe censorship so that nothing of an inflammatory, pro-Polish nature would incite audiences.

In spite of these and many other restrictions, the spirit of a free Poland continued to permeate the land, and nowhere did the flame burn more brightly than in Warsaw. Her citizens were so volatile that even the imperial Russian army would take no chances, and a regulation forbidding any two conscripts from Warsaw to serve in the same Russian company of troops was strictly observed.

Into this tightly controlled city came Lola Montez, pursuing recognition on the stage and the opportunity to earn a substantial living for herself there. We do not know whether her introduction to the manager of the Opera was arranged by her Prussian benefactor or whether she went on her own initiative. Few foreigners sought work at the Warsaw Opera, and this woman who claimed to be Spanish but spoke a far better English and French was a spectacularly attractive foreigner. As a dancer she would not be required to speak any lines, and she was hired as the prima ballerina of the opera company.

She made her first appearance in a comic opera by a young Italian composer, Giuseppe Verdi: *Un Giorno di Regno.* Although the work had been a failure when it was first presented at La Scala in Milan four years earlier, the ambitious Poles were reviving it under a new title, *Il Finto Stanislão,* and the composer had agreed to allow four performances. Unlike Verdi's other works, this light opera depended upon actors and dancers as well as singers, and the role of the prima ballerina was an important one. As luck had it, rehearsals were already under way when Lola was hired, with the opening scheduled to take place ten days later, on September 4.

The boldness—a modern writer might call it *chutzpah*—of the young Englishwoman was indisputable. Her career to date consisted of one performance on the London stage, which had ended in confusion and disgrace. Yet she unhesitatingly accepted a part—displacing an experienced dancer—that required a considerable professional skill. Convinced that hard work would overcome any technical handicaps, she threw herself into her role with a gusto that surprised the other members of the cast.

On the night of September 4, 1843, Lola finally achieved the great triumph she had been seeking. The audience gave her a standing ovation, and refused to allow her to leave the stage until she had taken seventeen curtain calls. Her dancing, to be sure, left much to be desired, but her beauty captivated her Polish audience, which was also quick to respond to her all but ferocious enthusiasm.

Without exception the seven newspapers then published in Warsaw praised Lola Montez in terms so lavish that they would have embarrassed a Pavlova. But Lola accepted the panegyrics as her due. One of the critics devoted more than three columns of a four-column review to a lyrical description of Lola's charms. He raved about her hair for three paragraphs, spent four more on her eyes, and even devoted two paragraphs to her teeth.

It did not matter, at least to the manager of the Opera, that his stars had been ignored, his superb singing chorus had received scant mention, or that only a few routine remarks had been made about Verdi. The prima ballerina was the sensation of the day, and the Opera's schedule was hastily revised so that the remaining three performances would take place within the next two weeks. Meanwhile, a hurried search was made for a musical work that would give the foreign dancer another opportunity to shine. No one seemed to notice that even the most overwhelmed of the critics confined themselves to a few noncommittal observations on the prima ballerina's dancing as such.

Lola gloried in her success but took care to preserve a modest front. Insisting that her small sitting room and bedchamber were adequate to her needs, she refrained from moving into larger lodgings—even though that sitting room was crowded day and night with Polish aristocrats, great ladies, and creative artists. Princes escorted her to performances of other operas, and leading members of Polish society gave dinner and supper parties in her honor. Crowds gathered in the street outside her flat to cheer her when she entered and departed, and the poets of Warsaw held a competition to determine which of them could write an ode that best captured her volatile spirit.

It was that spirit, above all, that was responsible for her triumph. Certainly her vivacity and exuberance were extraordinary, and the Poles were quick to appreciate these qualities.

Something else dawned more gradually on her Polish admirers. No Russians were seen with Lola either in public or in private. A number of members of the ruling hierarchy had called on her, as had several high-ranking Russian officers stationed in the Warsaw garrison; but whenever one of them asked for the privilege of acting as her escort, they would find she had made a previous engagement for the evening in question.

This attitude could not have been accidental. Lola proved all too often throughout her life that she was conscious of power centers, and she nearly always made it her business to work her way closer to them. In this situation, however, she deliberately chose to ally herself with the Poles rather than with their Russian masters.

This is not to say that she longed to help the cause of Polish freedom. On the other hand, those critics who later said she had been an opportunist trying to win cheap popularity by pretending she was a champion of a national spirit may have done her an injustice.

As her subsequent career in Bavaria would show, she was no liberal in the Western European sense. Her political attitudes are difficult to categorize as she moved from one country to another. A close examination of her conduct over the years does reveal, however, a fairly consistent concern for freedom.

At all times and in all things she was an advocate of total social equality for women; in this she stood with George Sand. Like Sand, too, she believed the time was not yet ripe for the participation of women in political affairs, although she naturally excluded herself from such prohibitions.

Her comments on the subject of her activities in Poland were almost exclusively personal, and her few political remarks, such as "The Poles dream of politics, not women," were open to a variety of interpretations. Because Lola was impulsive, her political comments sometimes seem erratic, but the positions she took over a period of many years suggest an underlying logic developed on her own initiative.

As she later hinted in an interview in the *Times* of London, she equated the position of the Poles under Russian rule with her own unenviable position as a woman trying to make her way in a world ruled by men. Just as she had to use underhanded means in attaining her ends, so would the Poles achieve freedom only by sawing obliquely at the chains clamped on them by Imperial Russia.

Whatever her motives, casting her lot with the Poles made Lola a national heroine in Poland. There are two conflicting stories on the subject, both told by Lola herself. Thanks to the rigid censorship of the press, neither of the alleged incidents ever reached the light of print.

One of the stories was Lola's original version, corroborated by the private correspondence of several Polish patriots, at least two of whom subsequently served prison terms in Siberia. The more believable of the stories, it was probably rejected later by Lola for the later, more sensational tale.

The management of the Warsaw Opera had found a new vehicle for the sensational foreign dancer—*Robert le Diable*, by the Italian-French composer Giacomo Meyerbeer. Initially presented twelve years earlier in Paris, *Robert* was a work that initiated the grand romantic tradition of opera, with a strong, melodramatic story and ballet music that were unique for the period.

There was a risk in scheduling *Robert le Diable,* since the story revolved around a strong ruler whose resemblance to a certain tyrant was evident. But the censors cleared the script for production, and the opening was scheduled for mid-October. Rehearsals began at once, and Lola plunged into her new role with characteristic enthusiasm.

Lola's role in *Robert le Diable* was larger than that in her initial triumph, and she even had a dramatic part to play. This caused some problems at the beginning of rehearsals: she was not a singer, and would obviously be made to look foolish by the others in the cast if she tried to sing. This dilemma was solved by allowing her to speak the lines.

Among those in the audience for the opera's first performance on October 16 was Baron General Paskievitch, the Russian Governor-General of Poland, who attended with all of the senior officials of his staff. They reacted favorably to the first two acts, and joined the rest of the audience in vigorously applauding each of Lola's appearances. She seemed well on her way to repeating her previous success.

Lola's longest speech was in the third act, and consisted of thirty or forty words. She was neither a professional actress as yet, nor even a talented amateur, but her beauty helped compensate for her lack of histrionic ability, and she managed well enough. She delivered the lines in a satisfactory manner and then added a few words of her own at the end:

"All people everywhere," she said, "demand the right to be free."

There was a moment of electric silence, followed by cheers and prolonged applause from the predominantly Polish audience.

Baron Paskievitch stared straight ahead, his arms folded; other Russians in the theater looked equally grim. For a moment the management feared that the Governor-General might walk out, which undoubtedly would mean the closing of the Opera the following day. But Paskievitch had no desire to draw further attention to the incident, and the performance continued.

That night Lola's Polish friends toasted her at a party given in her honor. Some of them warned her that the Russians could not allow the provocative addition to her speech to pass unchallenged, but she shrugged off their warnings.

The following morning she learned that the Russians were as sensitive as she had been advised. A check with the script had proved the line to be her own, and an aide to the Governor-General appeared at the door of her flat. When he asked her to accompany him to the office of Baron Paskievitch, Lola refused on the grounds that she had not yet made herself presentable.

The occupying authorities could not tolerate this defiance, and several hours later one of Lola's Polish admirers, who worked in the Ministry of the Interior, came to her with a warning that Russian troops were coming to her flat to take her into custody. Urged to flee, she rejected the idea, saying she would not take a coward's escape. Instead she procured two pistols from another Polish friend and returned to her flat to wait for the inevitable knock at her door.

When it came, and the colonel in command of the Russian detachment identified himself, Lola refused to open the door. The colonel retaliated by saying he would order it smashed in.

Lola informed him that it was the right of every woman to protect her honor, and said she would shoot the first Russian who set foot inside the flat.

A crowd had gathered in the street outside. The colonel was embarrassed. He had no desire to make a martyr of the headstrong dancer, and the sound of shots might spark a riot that could spread rapidly through the tense city. Trying to make the best of a delicate situation, he laid siege to the apartment.

Lola's predicament was even worse than anyone realized. There was a British Consul in Warsaw, but she could not appeal to him for protection without revealing her true identity. She had no Spanish passport, of course, and the possession of one would have done her no good since Spain had no consular representation in the city.

The problem was solved by the French Consul, a bachelor who happened to be one of Lola's admirers. Word of the dramatic confrontation spread quickly through Warsaw, and when the French official learned of her plight, he went immediately to her flat, obtained the Russians' permission to enter, and granted Lola immunity as a citizen of France and a subject of Louis Philippe.

This ended the incident. Lola was spared arrest, but the Russians could not risk a further outrage—they ordered her to leave Warsaw by the following morning, and a huge crowd was on hand to cheer her when she departed.

Neither then nor later did Lola explain why she had chosen to make the provocative remark from the stage of the Opera, and for many years she allowed the facts to speak for themselves. But by the time she wrote her autobiography two decades later, she had achieved an international reputation as a femme fatale, and it was perhaps to enhance this image that she wrote a new version of the Warsaw incident. On the morning after her performance, she said, she was summoned to the office of the Governor-General. Baron Paskievitch proclaimed that he admired her courage as well as her beauty, and suggested that she become his mistress, offering her a home in the country, jewels, and furs.

Lola, according to her autobiographical account, indignantly refused. The Governor-General tried to apply indirect pressure, and for the next few nights she was hissed by Russians in the audience whenever she appeared on the stage of the Opera. She, of course, remained steadfast in her determination to protect her honor, until Paskievitch finally lost his patience. He sent troops to take her into custody, she wrote—and then told the rest of the story in more or less the same form as the previous version.

Apparently it did not occur to her that she had diminished her own stature by making the change in the story. Perhaps she was misled by the fact that the Russians did not at any time regard her as a serious supporter of Polish liberty. They apparently assumed she had made her provocative remark impulsively and were ready to forget the entire matter.

In her autobiography Lola makes one error serious enough to cast doubt on every alleged fact in the book. From Warsaw, she wrote, she traveled to St. Petersburg, where she was received by

Tsar Nicholas I. It is unlikely in the extreme that a woman expelled by the Russian viceroy in Warsaw for inflammatory support of Polish political aspirations would have been permitted to make a visit to Russia. And even if the secret police slipped badly and allowed her inside the Russian capital, it is beyond credence that the Tsar—the man who had annexed Poland—would have granted an audience of any kind to someone who had just expressed public support of his foes.

It is true that Lola Montez paid a visit to St. Petersburg, but she did not go there until the following spring, when the Warsaw incident had been forgotten. Even then it is doubtful that she met the Tsar or that she engaged in a romance with him, as her autobiography hints. The supreme ruler of all the Russias was not in the habit of meeting foreign theatrical performers.

For the sake of the record, Lola spent an uneventful two or three weeks in St. Petersburg. If she had any hope of dancing there, she soon abandoned it. Ballet had already achieved a standing as the highest of the interpretative arts in Russia, and had an impresario been mad enough to hire her, she would have been laughed off any stage in the sophisticated city, where every nuance of a dancer's performance was noted and appreciated.

So the stories Lola told of her friendship with the Tsar must be discounted *in toto*. Oddly enough, she displayed rare circumspection in discussing a liaison with another of Europe's most celebrated men that actually *did* happen not long after she left Warsaw.

[CHAPTER V]

There is no record anywhere, other than Lola's fabrication of a trip to St. Petersburg, regarding her whereabouts during the final months of 1843. After her expulsion from Warsaw, she appears to have vanished for twelve weeks. She may have accompanied some man on his travels, for she could hardly have afforded a holiday on her own. She had been well paid by the Warsaw Opera, but she had spent freely, too, and her funds were low. It seems reasonable to assume that an admirer paid most of her bills during this period.

Early in 1844, the year in which she celebrated her twenty-sixth birthday, Lola Montez suddenly appeared in Dresden and fell in love with Franz Liszt. Perhaps she was ready for her first real love affair—even an adventuress might be vulnerable to the grand passion. And few women living in the middle of the nineteenth century could have resisted the overwhelming attractions of the man and the city in which their romance took place.

"Liszt," Balzac wrote, "has made Europe aware of his native Hungary." The great French author was inclined to exaggeration, but in this instance he was telling the precise truth.

Liszt had created a sensation throughout the Continent when he played his first concert in Vienna at the age of eleven. Now, twenty-two years later, the composer-pianist had achieved great fame. His skill as a performing artist was so extraordinary that, it was said, he composed only because he could not show off his technique sufficiently playing the works of other composers. The common people everywhere loved him for his tireless championing of personal liberties, and his performances were so brilliant that kings and cabinet ministers often presented him with expensive gifts. These he promptly gave to the poor.

He was universally regarded as a romantic figure, principally because of his affair with Marie d'Agoult, a beautiful French noblewoman who had deserted her husband for him and given him three children. That she became the literary rival of their friend George Sand and wrote a number of successful books under the pen name of Daniel Stern only added to Liszt's luster.

Liszt's reputation as a lover was formidable. He left trails of broken hearts behind him on his concert tours, and his understanding of feminine psychology was rumored to be so great that no woman had the strength to refuse him. He was exceptionally handsome, almost beautiful, with a fair skin, curly hair, and eyes so expressive that several of his mistresses later claimed he had hypnotized them.

Dresden was a city that exerted its own charms. A community of approximately one-third of a million people at the time of Lola's visit, the capital of Saxony stood second only to Vienna as a center of the arts in the German-speaking world. Situated on the winding banks of the Elbe River, and the principal crossroads in both east-west and north-south traffic, it wielded an influence far out of proportion to its size. Young artists, authors, and composers from many countries had congregated there for centuries, and countless trends in the arts had been Dresden-inspired.

Thanks to this artistic heritage, the people of Dresden were more cosmopolitan than were those of many larger towns. An author seeking an appropriate setting in which to write a novel or epic poem came to Dresden for the purpose, as did dramatists, composers, and painters.

Franz Liszt had come to the city for a series of concerts early in 1844 and, finding the atmosphere to his liking, had canceled the rest of his tour and taken an apartment where he could compose music and rest after his travels. Lola Montez arrived at about the same time, seeking work as a dancer in one of Dresden's many theaters. How they met is a matter of conjecture, although they must have known many of the same people.

What is significant is Lola's treatment of Liszt in her autobiography. She claims the scalps of many men who were mere acquaintances, but she barely admits that she met Liszt and heard one of his concerts. She says not one word about their romance.

Almost immediately after her arrival in Munich in January of 1844, she obtained an engagement as a dancer at the Court Theatre. Her Saxon audiences recognized her ineptitude for what it was, but her beauty, as usual, made a firm impression, and she was very well received. She was paid high wages, worked four nights each week, and took lodgings in a small residential hotel overlooking the river. Admirers thronged her sitting room, but she held them at a distance.

According to Liszt's correspondence, Lola attended the last of the three concerts he had scheduled in Dresden, and they met soon thereafter, perhaps at one of the parties given by patrons of the arts. By that time he had made up his mind to remain in the city for a time, and had already either canceled or postponed the remainder of his tour.

Hindsight makes it logical that Lola Montez and Franz Liszt should have been attracted to each other. He was tired of the adulation of ordinary women, just as she was bored by the attentions of ordinary men. Both Lola and Liszt were aware of their respective charms and automatically expected to be the center of interest wherever they went. Even more important, both were individualists who could not respect authority for its own sake. Lola sought the freedom of women, and Liszt dreamed of liberty for all mankind.

On a deeper psychological basis their romance was equally well grounded. Liszt could develop a real interest in a woman only if she was strong-minded as well as beautiful, intelligent as well as charming. And Lola, never really having known a man who appreciated her mind, was discovering the joys of relationships that were cerebral as well as physical.

A few days after Liszt's final concert, he withdrew into his suite at the Alberthaus, the finest of Dresden's old hotels, and made himself unavailable to local society. His neighbors could hear him playing his piano at different times of the day, and at noon, weather permitting, he went out for a two-hour walk along the river. The rest of his time was spent in isolation. His meals were brought to his suite, and he ate alone, the hotel's waiters reporting that he usually read while consuming his food.

His hermitlike existence lasted no more than a week. Rumors began to fly: the spectacularly lovely Spanish dancer from the Court Theatre had joined him for dinner in his suite one evening and was still there for breakfast the next morning. Soon it was common knowledge that Lola Montez had moved in with Liszt.

Lola kept her own flat and spent several hours there each day she performed at the theater; otherwise she lived with Liszt at the Alberthaus. They made no attempt to keep their affair secret, and Lola accompanied him on his daily walks. After a week or two they began to appear together at inns and restaurants, and when Lola assumed a new dancing role at the Court Theatre, the composer-pianist was present in a box for her first performance.

News of the affair traveled swiftly, soon reaching the ears of Liszt's friend George Sand in Paris. "I am told," she wrote, "that Liszt is much enamored of a Spanish lady in Dresden, the daughter of a grandee who lives in reduced circumstances. She is incomparably beautiful, and I am informed that our handsome Marie would look plain if they could be persuaded to stand side by side. This will not happen, to be sure, so at least some portion of Marie's reputation will be salvaged."

There were many Parisians who would have taken pleasure in telling Marie d'Agoult about her lover's latest liaison, but none more than George Sand, who was now on the worst of terms with the woman who had been her intimate friend. There was no direct contact between the two, but it would have been an easy matter for Sand to make certain that the story reached its mark.

In any event Marie d'Agoult did hear the story, whereupon she wrote a bitterly reproachful letter to Liszt. It was not the first letter of this sort she had sent him; he usually replied by denying solemnly that he had been unfaithful to her. Knowing him, she would understand that this was his way of signaling to her that his current affair was of no consequence, and she would drop the subject.

In this instance, however, Liszt neither denied nor confirmed Marie's accusations. She and the children were always present in his thoughts, he wrote her, and he was looking forward to the day when they would be reunited in Paris. At present he was enjoying his rest and believed he would feel refreshed when he resumed his concert tour.

His failure to answer Marie's charges inspired an even stronger letter, in which she made the mistake of appealing to his intellect. Again Liszt replied blandly, and without so much as admitting that such a person as Lola Montez existed. "Various ladies here flirt with me, of course," he wrote, "but the Germans are so clumsy in matters of sentiment that I laugh behind their backs."

For all his evasions in letters to his principal mistress, Franz Liszt made no serious attempt to keep his affair with Lola Montez a secret from the rest of the world. They appeared together at art galleries, and at churches, in some of which Liszt was persuaded by the pastor to try out the organ. They attended the theater; they dined in restaurants with their heads close together; they accepted local invitations and gave a number of small dinner parties in Liszt's rooms at the Alberthaus.

At one such affair they met the new British military attaché in the legation accredited to the court of Frederick Augustus II, the Elector of Saxony. He was a lieutenant colonel who had recently been transferred from the Indian Army, and Lola had known him well in Calcutta. He looked puzzled for a moment when he was presented to her, as though trying to recall where they had met.

But he quickly accepted her new identity, even though she addressed him in English. Presumably she took care to emphasize her Spanish accent.

Stories continued to reach Paris that Liszt's affair with Lola was of serious proportions. They exchanged gold signet rings and other tokens, and when Lola called in a dressmaker to create a new wardrobe for her, Liszt paid the bill. They seemed inseparable; only when Lola was at work in the theater were they ever seen apart.

The lovers lived in a time when virtually everyone who was literate wrote letters, but they exchanged virtually no correspondence—presumably because they spent so much of their time together. In any event, only a few scraps have ever been found.

One, dated February 11, 1844, was written by Lola. "I will not tolerate tyranny," she wrote Liszt. "If you change your mind, you will find me at my lodgings." The cold note was signed L.M.

The cause of their quarrel is unknown, but it soon blew over, and Lola moved back into Liszt's suite. They remained together until late March, and although details are lacking, it is reasonable to assume that the road of love was filled with ruts. Both were temperamental, both were demanding, and neither was accustomed to giving in to the whims of other people. Whatever their difficulties, after a liaison that had lasted almost three months, they abruptly parted company late in March, 1844.

Which of them was responsible for the break is difficult to determine. Two very different stories have been told, and as no documentary evidence has ever been offered to substantiate either, it is almost impossible to decide which, if either, is true.

Several of Lola's early biographers claimed that she stormed out of Liszt's Alberthaus suite after an explosive argument and did not return. Within a day or two she left her position at the Court Theatre and went on to Paris, while Liszt, departing from Dresden at the same time, went to Berlin to resume his concert tour.

A second story, also attributed to some of Lola's biographers, indicates that it was Liszt who made the break. The pair quarreled one afternoon, and when the issue remained unresolved, Lola announced she was going into her bedroom in the suite for a nap. According to this account, Liszt packed his belongings while Lola slept and then fled by carriage, taking care to pay the hotel manager in advance for the furniture he knew Lola would break when she awakened to find him gone.

A third account, found in the correspondence of Victor Hugo, who was the composer's friend, may be nearer the truth than either of these versions. Lola and Liszt, who had quarreled on a number of occasions, could not reconcile their differences. Since both of them knew they were living in a glare of publicity, they decided to break off in such a manner as to hold scandal to a minimum. Lola's engagement at the Court Theatre was coming to its end, so she and Liszt arranged to travel together to Paris. This they did, immediately going their separate ways when they reached the city.

Of far greater importance is the fact that Lola Montez had enjoyed her first genuine romance. She may have been no more than a passing fancy in the life of Liszt, but she had learned love from him. It might even be argued that Franz Liszt changed the direction of Lola's life. Necessity had encouraged her to live as an opportunist ever since returning to England from India, and for portions of that time she had supported herself as a courtesan, however high-priced.

After Liszt, most of her affairs would be of longer duration—and, presumably, more meaningful. She would concentrate on one man at a time, developing a genuine interest in him before circumstances or her own nature terminated the relationship. It is easy to exaggerate the effect of Liszt's influence on Lola, but unquestionably she was softer and more feminine in her subsequent affairs and marriages.

On the other hand, she was so energetic, so narcissistic, and so insistent in her demands that she be granted the same freedoms her lovers enjoyed—a revolutionary doctrine for the time—that it seems unlikely she could have found any one man with whom she could be happy for the rest of her days.

It is not enough to say that Lola was restless, that her nature demanded excitement and change. Never having known parental love, she made emotional claims on her lovers and husbands that no one man could have fulfilled for long.

Liszt's description of her was crisp in a brief comment he made in a letter to George Sand: "The Spanish lady," he wrote, "was like the wind that unleashes a sea of sand and dirt on the plains of Castile and leaves one red-eyed and spent when it has passed."

[CHAPTER VI]

If London was the most civilized of Western cities, Paris was the most urbane, the fastest-paced, the most challenging. The ferment there—churnings and eruptions and changes—was evident in the arts, in industry, in politics in the growing class struggle, and even in theology. No one stood still, no two men thought alike, and to agree on anything was as difficult for working class men as it was for intellectuals.

The government of Louis Philippe was becoming increasingly repressive just at a time when liberals and radicals were demanding greater freedom, and there were many who believed a new civil war to be imminent. The Industrial Revolution was relatively slow in reaching France, but the middle class continued to grow in influence and power as well as wealth, and many of the bourgeoisie felt themselves trapped between the conservatism of the entrenched aristocracy and the yearnings of the working class for a share in the good things of life.

In the world of literature, it was said, classicism was dead; but no one had bothered to give it a decent burial. Victor Hugo had led the swing toward romanticism, Honoré de Balzac and his followers were realists, and every conceivable style was being tried as well. The theater was booming, and as many as fifty playhouses were open to accommodate the growing crowds. Newspapers proliferated, new magazines appeared every month and sometimes every week, and new book-publishing firms sprang into existence to meet the demands of an increasingly literate public.

Visitors soon discovered the truth of Balzac's observation that there was not one Paris but many. The monarchists who still sat in the seats of power rarely appeared in public, seldom made their views known, and conducted their social lives behind the closed doors of their mansions. The middle class still reflected the quiet, almost backward conservatism of the provinces, but new ideas were germinating as discontent with the status quo became increasingly widespread. The poor—the grandsons of the men who had created the French Revolution, the sons of the men who had filled the ranks of Napoleon's great legions—were growing restless and impatient for the long-promised day when they would enjoy the fruits of liberty, equality, and fraternity.

The creative and interpretative artists who reflected these views, giving them shape, substance, and direction, were a class apart. Their standards of morality and ethics were exclusively their own· they lived as they pleased, making and breaking their own rules within their own circles while trying not to overstep the bounds of propriety that separated them from the rest of Paris.

In April, 1844, Lola Montez became a probationary member of this special band. The Opera was her first target, and her success in Warsaw and Dresden made it easy for her to obtain work there. She was hired to dance the role of the prima ballerina in a two-act opera by Halevy, *Il Lazzerone*, which was presented late in the month.

The Paris audience was a critical one, rewarding the deserving with generous applause and the incompetent with disdain. After Lola danced in the first act, they sat on their hands, and only her quick thinking, combined with a stroke of good luck, saved her from disaster. As she was concluding her performance, one of her satin slippers fell off, and the audience began to laugh. Reacting quickly, she threw the slipper to a handsome gentleman seated in a box, following the gesture by blowing him a kiss before she sank into a deep curtsy. Parisians admired wit as much as they respected talent, and they paid tribute to the beautiful woman's presence of mind by giving her a prolonged round of applause. The critics were less generous in the next morning's papers.

The *Constitutionnel,* one of the more highly regarded newspapers, chided her gently: "We would like to warn young dancers against the dangers of allowing applause spurred by causes unrelated to their dancing to go to their heads. At the same time we feel compelled to abstain from criticizing too severely a pretty young woman who has not yet had time to study Parisian tastes."

La Presse was a far less influential journal, but the comments of its reviewer are of interest because of the reviewer himself. In time Théophile Gautier, now in his early thirties, would become the leading literary and theatrical critic of his time. An intimate friend of Hugo, Balzac, and other literary giants of the age, he was himself a poet, dramatist, and essayist of distinction. A burly, handsome man with an eye for beauty and a hatred of sham, he was merciless in his assault:

> We are reluctant to speak of Lola Montes [sic], who reminds us by her Christian name of one of the prettiest women of Granada, and by her surname of the man who excited in us the most powerful dramatic emotions we have ever experienced—Montes, the most illustrious *espada* of Spain. The only thing Andalusian about Mlle. Lola Montes is her magnificent mane of auburn hair; even her eyes are unlike those ever seen in Spain, remarkable though they may be. She gabbles Spanish very indifferently, English passably, and her French is scarcely much better, though one must admit she has an ear for the finer nuances of our language.
>
> Which is her country? That is the question, and Mlle. Montes, one must assume, is in no hurry to answer it. Very well then, she forces us to discuss her other attributes. We may say that Mlle. Lola has a very small foot and unusually pretty legs. Her use of these is another matter.
>
> The curiosity excited by her adventures with the Russian police in Poland, and her recent romance with a musical artist of rare talent, has not been satisfied, it must be admitted. Mlle. Lola Montes is certainly inferior to Dolores Serrai, who has, at least, the advantage of being a real Spaniard, and redeems her imperfections as a dancer by a voluptuous abandon, and an admirable fire and precision of rhythm. We are informed by the representa-

tives of the Opera that their new ballerina has many exploits as an equestrienne to her credit, and we suspect that Mlle. Lola is more at home in the saddle than on the boards.

Gautier's cruelty was echoed by most of the other critics, and the Opera decided not to avail itself further of Lola's talents. Lola, as impervious to the critics as she was beautiful, had no difficulty in finding other employment in a city that, more than any other, put a premium on beauty for its own sake. Within a few days Lola was hired as a prima ballerina by the Porte Saint Martin, a theater that specialized in the presentation of light and comic operas. Its standards, obviously, were less rigorous than those of the Opera.

A different musical play was presented at the Porte Saint Martin each evening, the total repertory consisting of about fifteen works. The choreography for these light operas was indifferently planned, the attention of the principal players being directed toward singing and acting. It was therefore unnecessary for Lola to prepare in depth for any single role. She was allowed to improvise, which gave her the opportunity to dance as she pleased.

Clever enough to have taken the *Constitutionnel's* words to heart, she made it her business to find out what Parisians liked to watch. Results came quickly and she achieved a success sufficient to win her a place in the city's community of creative and interpretative artists.

Gautier was to change his tune after he came to know Lola. Taken by her beauty and charm, he praised her in five or six different articles for her delicacy, grace, stage presence, and beauty. Unable to say anything positive about her dancing, he made no mention of her actual performance.

The authors, editors, and actors of Paris were not slow to note the arrival of a spectacularly attractive young woman in their midst, and Lola was inundated with invitations to dinners and suppers. By now she had learned how severely she would be judged in any community by the company she kept, and she accepted no invitations until she could sort out her would-be swains.

The first escort with whom she made a public appearance was

Eugene Sue, the novelist. Sue was riding a high wave of popularity: the serialized versions of his books were not only accounting for enormous increases in the circulation of the newspapers in which they appeared, but he was said to be earning even more than the prolific Balzac from these sales. Solvent, socially acceptable, and impeccably tailored, he had acquired a reputation for squiring the most beautiful women around Paris. Among them were actresses, at least one author, and several courtesans, all of whom had one virtue in common: they were exceptionally pretty.

Lola had made a shrewd choice, for being seen with Sue immediately enhanced her reputation as a beauty. Some of her early biographers have claimed that she was Sue's mistress for a time, but there is no verification for the story. It did not necessarily follow that Lola was sleeping with Sue merely because he escorted her to the theater and to supper. In fact, it is probable that, considering the care Lola was taking to protect her reputation, she did not become his mistress.

The next man to seek Lola's company was the elder Alexandre Dumas, and it is a fact that she appeared at a number of the parties he gave in his large flat. Lola herself is the authority for the statement that Dumas was not her lover. Certainly it would have been impossible for her not to have known of his extraordinary reputation as a Lothario. Countless jokes were told in Parisian literary and theatrical circles about the prowess of Dumas and Victor Hugo, all variations on the same theme—a mythical competition for the favor of young women. Behind this humor there was a kernel of truth: both of these renowned authors seemed to have insatiable appetites, and both engaged in endless sexual adventures. Hugo, it was said, took his girls wherever he found them and was indifferent to their origins, enjoying a streetwalker as readily as a young lady of the aristocracy. Dumas, although no more particular than his friend, specialized in actresses, singers, dancers, and young women who had theatrical aspirations. One joke had it that Dumas wrote for the theater from time to time only because his activities as a playwright gave him access to more girls.

There could be no doubt that a young woman lost her reputation if she was seen frequently in the company of the overweight, good-natured Dumas, so Lola Montez was very careful. Others were always present when she attended functions at Dumas', and she saw to it that someone escorted her to her own flat before the party ended. When she allowed Dumas to take her to supper, they sat at a table with his friends and colleagues. At no time was she alone with him.

In spite of her caution, however, she relished her life in the bohemian world of Paris. Here she found kindred spirits, people whose standards were remarkably similar to her own. Of far greater significance to Lola was her acceptance as the equal of the men she met. She stood on her own small feet as a dancer, no matter how unimpressive her talents, and no man looked down on her because of her sex.

During this period Lola met Aurore Dudevant, the heiress who had achieved literary renown and personal notoriety as George Sand. Lola not only visited the most successful, independent woman of the age at her Paris flat, but spent at least one weekend at the Dudevant country estate, where other prominent figures also gathered.

Like everyone else in Paris, George Sand was struck by the beauty of the new arrival, but Lola's mind failed to make an impression on her. "There may be no one in Paris prettier than our little Spanish dancer," she wrote to her son, Maurice, "but she tries in vain to understand matters beyond her grasp. Alas! no one person can be both a Cleopatra and an Aristotle."

Lola knew the most famous Frenchwoman of the century at a time when George Sand's involvement in politics was as deep as her commitment to literature. This interest, it might be noted, continued to absorb her until she became disillusioned while holding the equivalent of a cabinet position in the Provisional Republican government during the revolution of 1848. A number of sources have long put forth the claim that Lola's own involvement in the politics of Bavaria was sparked by her acquaintance with George Sand.

The facts suggest coincidence, nothing more. At the time Lola and George Sand knew each other in 1844, Sand could not have anticipated acquiring power and prestige in her own right. She wrote a number of newspaper articles in which she argued the cause of socialism, but her stance was strictly that of an intellectual debating her peers. It is also true that she was never closely associated with Lola Montez. It would be stretching the truth to say they were friends; George Sand's hospitality was extended to the younger woman principally because Lola's escort on one occasion or another happened to be a member of the Sand circle.

For the first five months of Lola's life in Paris, she tried conscientiously to improve her skill as a dancer. Her efforts were rewarded by two increases in wages, but she splurged on new clothes and saved very little money. Lola was a woman who instinctively knew how to express her personality through her attire; the letters of virtually everyone who knew her mention her stunning gowns and accessories. Her primary aim was to promote Lola Montez, building her image until she won recognition as a theatrical star.

If anyone inspired her it was an actress, Marie Dorval, who long had been known as the most beautiful woman in France. For many years the mistress of poet Alfred de Vigny, and for at least part of that time George Sand's lover, Mme. Dorval was a mediocre actress whose beauty and grace on a stage caused critics and audiences alike to overlook how much her talent left to be desired.

What one beauty had done, another could emulate. Lola set her goal, and began to work toward it. Her plans were disrupted by the least expected of developments: she fell in love again. As she herself admitted in later years, the relationship was unique in her long history of romances and affairs.

[CHAPTER VII]

In the mid-1840's the loveliest and most charming woman in Paris—and therefore, in the opinion of French intellectuals, in the world—was a courtesan named Olympe Pelissier. She was so beautiful and such a delightful companion that she found herself in the unusual position of making her own choices from the scores of prominent men who sought her favors. For a few years she allowed herself to be kept by Eugene Sue, but her relationship with him was by no means exclusive. The novelist had first call on Olympe's time, to be sure, and she was seen with him at the theater, the opera, and at restaurants. But their liaison did not prevent her from making public appearances with other men or entertaining them in private at her apartment overlooking the Seine.

Honoré de Balzac took Sue's position with Olympe as a challenge, and this shrewd young blonde allowed herself to be seen with him, too, although some authorities doubt that they had an affair. Delacroix proclaimed Olympe too beautiful to be captured on canvas. Victor Hugo dedicated a poem to her but carefully refrained from starting an affair—he preferred obscure mistresses.

The paths of Lola Montez and Olympe Pelissier crossed soon after Lola's arrival on the Parisian social scene in 1844. According to the elder Alexandre Dumas, Lola immediately regarded the other beauty as a rival to be dethroned. Olympe enjoyed a number of advantages, among them the money to buy clothes, which enabled her to boast with some accuracy that she was the best-dressed woman in Paris. She was condescendingly polite to the newcomer, and it may have been this attitude more than anything else that inspired Lola to inaugurate her campaign to displace Olympe.

Claudin, a wit who knew everybody and had kind words for none, duly noted in his correspondence the appearance of Lola Montez on the Parisian scene:

At last there has arrived in the city one who will challenge the supremacy of the immortal Olympe, and I am safe in predicting she cannot wait to do battle with the queen of the boulevards. Lola Montez is an enchantress. There is something about her, something provoking and voluptuous, which draws all men to her. Her skin is white, her wavy hair like the tendrils of the woodbine, her eyes tameless and wild, her mouth like a budding pomegranate. Add to that a dashing figure, charming feet, and perfect grace.

Alas, as a dancer she has no talent. But no matter—her presence makes Paris a livelier place, and Olympe, who has recognized no rivals, hates her with a malice that is almost frightening to behold. The months that lie ahead promise much amusement to observers of the passing scene.

Lola served notice on the empress of the demimonde that she was in earnest by snaring one of Olympe's lovers, the celebrated Joseph Mery, who at the time was regarded as one of the foremost poets and literary critics in France. Mery was middle-aged and overweight, but neither his appearance nor his age discouraged Lola from using him to sharpen her talents as a man-stealer.

Mery remained on friendly terms with Olympe to the extent that they spoke when they met in public, but he soon established Lola in a small but comfortable Left Bank apartment not far from his own dwelling. Their relationship was similar to the one Olympe enjoyed with Eugene Sue: Mery had first call on Lola's time and services, but she was free to develop other friendships as she saw fit. This comfortable arrangement began early in 1845; and, as Lola was to put it in her *Autobiography*, she believed at the time that she would be content to build her new life on this foundation.

Her ambition, as it turned out, was too great to accept such a position, while Olympe Pelissier gloried in hers. Lola studied Olympe's admirers and set her sights on a natural target, Mery's friend Alexandre Henri Dujarier. Only a year or two older than Lola, Dujarier was wealthy, exceptionally handsome, talented, and a major power in the Paris Lola was determined to conquer.

Dujarier owned a half interest in the newspaper with the largest circulation in France, *La Presse*, although he left the active management in the hands of his partner, Émile de Girardin, a young financial genius who was rapidly building a journalistic empire. Dujarier also held a full-time position as the newspaper's literary critic and Lola, of course, was anxious to win the approval of the Paris newspapers. She saw Dujarier on a number of occasions, usually at the Café de Paris or at Hugo's favorite Grand Vefour restaurant. Sometimes Dujarier was escorting Olympe, whom he visited on Tuesdays and Fridays, but Lola felt certain from the way he looked at her that his ties to Olympe were breakable.

Lola made it her business to find out what she could about Dujarier's habits and, as Joseph Mery later admitted, it was he who inadvertently passed along most of the information that would result in the end of his own affair with Lola. Among other things, Mery told Lola that Dujarier went horseback riding every morning of his life, regardless of the weather. Lola checked for herself, sitting behind a veil in a carriage parked outside Dujarier's flat. After following him for several mornings, she knew his routes.

The rest was easy. A fine horsewoman, Lola rented a mount and "accidentally" met Dujarier on one of his postdawn rides. Within a day or two they were riding together every morning, at which point it seemed only natural for Dujarier to ask the Spanish dancer to accompany him to the theater and supper.

In less than two weeks from the time Lola first encountered Dujarier on his morning ride, she moved into his apartment. The gossips of Paris had no peers in the art of spotting romance, but this was one affair that had developed fully before a single hint appeared in print.

The first to learn of the romance was Mery, who promptly returned to Olympe Pelissier's fold. Olympe thus regained one of her lovers while losing another, but the exchange of the corpulent Mery for young Alexandre Dujarier was at best a poor bargain for a woman whose glamorous image was her livelihood. Under the circumstances it is not surprising that Lola's rival kept silent.

Alexandre Dumas heard of the new liaison from Dujarier, who was a good friend and who, fortunately, recorded the details. It was he who first spread the word that Lola and Dujarier were in love.

Paris would have guessed as much when Lola transferred all of her belongings to Dujarier's flat and set up housekeeping with him there. Although the atmosphere in French artistic circles was permissive, affairs were always conducted within the bounds of established customs—which Lola and Dujarier violated. When a man took a mistress, it was expected that he would establish her in a place of her own. Depending on the nature of their relationship, she would either be faithful to him or would openly continue to see other men. But no man of stature gave a mistress residence under his own roof unless the affair was more than an affair. Dujarier was notifying Paris that he was forsaking all others for a long time to come.

Attempts have been made over the years to find hidden reasons for Dujarier's actions, but the elder Dumas, his confidant, has it that he fell deeply in love with Lola. Dumas' correspondence also indicates that Lola told him the truth about her background and that Dujarier didn't care what she had been. A man expected his mistress to be lovely, charming, and at least occasionally passionate, but the young Frenchman discovered that Lola had a sharp mind, too, and the combination apparently overwhelmed him.

As for Lola, she also seems to have fallen in love, and in the process spoiled all of the careful plans she had made for her future in Paris. She no longer wanted fame or riches; she even put aside her desire to influence others. Apparently nothing mattered to her but the love she and Dujarier shared. Early biographers who viewed the affair as an attempt on Lola's part to win power through the half-owner of *La Presse* may have been quite simply mistaken. No one has ever been able to determine for certain whether Lola and Dujarier were using each other or were really in love, and the question mark makes their romance all the more piquant.

The correspondence of Dumas, Mery, and the justly indignant Olympe Pelissier seems to corroborate Lola's claim that she and Dujarier planned to be married. (She was not, of course, eligible, the London court having granted her husband a separation rather than an outright divorce.) Many of Dujarier's friends found it difficult to believe that he would risk his social standing by marrying a courtesan, but at this point public opinion meant as little to him as it did to Lola.

The wife of Emile Girardin, having acquired a reputation as the best hostess in Paris, gave a large dinner party for the betrothed couple. In doing so, she jeopardized their own social standing, but the Girardins were too wealthy and powerful to worry.

Lola and Dujarier, unmindful of the furor they were creating, told their friends they would be married in the late spring and go to Spain for a honeymoon. Mery, who was Dujarier's friend and who was on good terms with Lola now, suggested that he accompany them—he had long been anxious to visit Spain. Lola and Dujarier agreed. The three of them knew, of course, that even the most permissive Parisians would be scandalized if the bride's former lover acted as chaperon, and common sense came at least halfway to the rescue. Mery had no intention of abandoning the journey, but it was arranged that Alexandre Dumas would join the party as well.

While Dujarier was enjoying the love of his mistress and happily making plans for their future, other aspects of his life were becoming complicated. A year or two before he had sold a half-interest in *La Presse* to Girardin, a former employee named Granier de Cassagnac had borrowed a substantial sum of money from him and, ungratefully, had founded a rival newspaper, the *Globe*. Now, with the repayment of the loan badly overdue, Dujarier, following the custom of the time, launched a personal attack in the columns of *La Presse* on his fellow journalist.

Taking up the banner on behalf of de Cassagnac was his dashing young brother-in-law from Guadeloupe, Jean Baptiste Rosemond de Beauvallon, who had some reasons of his own to enter the lists. Beauvallon was the *Globe*'s drama critic. Having been presented to Lola some weeks earlier, he had entertained hopes of striking up an affair with her. Now, thanks to her love for Dujarier, she would not so much as look at him.

Beauvallon's counterattack on Dujarier in the *Globe* unexpectedly brought a handsome young woman to his door. A Mme. Albert, she called herself a widow and told Beauvallon she had been engaged to marry Dujarier and had been jilted by him when he fell in love with Lola Montez. Madame Albert and Beauvallon soon began an affair of their own, but both wanted revenge and each goaded the other to it. The stage was set for a dramatic interlude.

Lola, meanwhile, was discovering that living as a wife in all but name was getting boring. Dujarier spent hours at his office each day, leaving her with nothing to do but sit around the apartment and await his return. Even though she would soon be a married woman, she decided it would be unwise to give up her career; Dujarier, who sought her happiness above all else, helped her obtain a new theatrical engagement. The previous damning reviews notwithstanding, she was signed as the prima ballerina for a new musical comedy, *La Biche au bois*, to be presented at the Porte-Saint-Martin Theatre. On March 1, 1845, she began rehearsals.

A few days later she and Dujarier were invited to a supper party to be held at the Frères Provençaux, a restaurant in the Palais Royal reputed to be the site of orgies attended by some of the wealthiest young men in town. These stories were somewhat exaggerated, as Dujarier well knew, having attended a number of suppers there, but several of Paris' more prominent courtesans had been asked to the party, and Dujarier did not want his future wife to be seen in their company.

Lola, who loved any kind of party, begged him to let her attend. Dujarier would not grant his permission, and his refusal sparked their first and only quarrel. Not only was Lola forbidden to go; Dujarier added insult to injury by dropping in at the affair himself. Unsettled by the quarrel with Lola, he drank too much champagne and became embroiled in an argument with Beauvallon, who was also a guest, heaping insults on him. Beauvallon astonished his friends by simply listening to Dujarier's charges.

When Dujarier returned home to his apartment later that night, he and Lola made up their differences. As far as Dujarier was concerned, the quarrel and party were over and done with. The next morning, March 12, he learned that Beauvallon had not forgotten the incident of the night before. Two gentlemen presented themselves to him as Beauvallon's seconds and, in their friend's name, challenged him to a duel. Dujarier realized, too late, that he had played into the hands of his enemies.

Beauvallon was known as one of the best pistol shots in France. He had won a number of shooting competitions, and he was also an accomplished swordsman, who kept in trim by spending several hours each week fencing. Dueling was illegal; had Dujarier kept his head, he would have refused the challenge and let himself be branded a coward by his opponents. Instead he accepted and, given the choice of weapons, elected pistols, being better acquainted with firearms than with the blade.

That evening, before Lola left for her rehearsals at the theater, Dujarier's seconds called on him to make the final arrangements for the fight. He was so preoccupied that Lola felt uneasy, but Dujarier persuaded her to leave. When he called for her later in the evening, she was even more convinced that something was wrong. She finally persuaded him to tell her at least part of the truth. He admitted that he was fighting a duel the next day. Not wanting Lola to worry, he told her his opponent would be the middle-aged Roger de Veauvoir. Both would fire harmless shots into the air, he said, and with honor on both sides satisfied, that would be the end of the matter.

Before the couple retired for the night, Alexandre Dumas came to Dujarier's flat, bringing with him a pair of new dueling pistols. Assuming Lola to be asleep in the adjoining room, the author tried to persuade his friend to give up the duel. Dujarier refused. If he backed out now, he said, he would be branded as a coward for the rest of his days.

Lola heard every word of the conversation. Realizing that Dujarier had been trying to protect her from the truth, she pretended to be asleep. Later, after Dumas had gone, she crept to the door of the living room and saw Dujarier seated at his desk, writing. Although she did not know it then, he was preparing his new will and writing notes to her and to his mother.

Instead of coming to her when he was finished, Dujarier went off to another bedroom and locked the door behind him.

Lola spent a miserable night, watched snow falling at dawn, and then asked the maid who brought her breakfast to her room to tell Dujarier she wanted to see him. Instead, the maid brought her a note:

> *My Dear Lola,*
>
> I am going out at once to fight a duel with pistols. This will explain why I wished to pass the night alone, and why I cannot come in to see you this morning. I need all the composure at my command, and you would have excited too much emotion in me.
>
> I will be with you at two o'clock this afternoon, unless—.
>
> Goodbye, my dear little Lola, the dear little girl I love.
>
> D.

According to Dumas' account, Lola rushed into the living room, where she found a copy of Dujarier's new will—he had taken another copy with him to give to Dumas. When she saw that he had left his entire estate to her, she burst into tears. Dressing hastily, she hurried to Dumas' apartment, hoping to prevent the duel. The servants there told her that Dumas had already gone and, following his instructions, said they did not know where he could be reached. The seconds, too, had left their homes, and no one knew where to find them.

Lola could do nothing but return to Dujarier's apartment and wait.

[CHAPTER VIII]

It was many hours before Lola learned what happened that morning in a secluded area deep in the Bois de Boulogne. Dujarier, his seconds, and Alexandre Dumas arrived at 8:30 A.M. Shortly thereafter the physician on whom the seconds for both principals had agreed, a Dr. de Guise, reached the scene. The event was scheduled for 9 A.M., but the hour came and went.

The morning was bitterly cold, with a few snowflakes drifting down, and by 10 A.M. the tense Dujarier was so chilled that Dr. de Guise pronounced him in no condition to fight a duel.

Dumas and the seconds tried their best to persuade Dujarier to leave. He had waited a full hour beyond the agreed time. His honor was satisfied, they insisted; no one could accuse him of cowardice in refusing to wait any longer. Dujarier listened to their arguments and paid no attention to them.

Dumas was still arguing with him when a carriage was heard moving down a path through the woods, and a short time later Beauvallon appeared with his party. His seconds apologized for their tardiness, but Beauvallon himself took no notice of anyone. He stood with his arms folded, staring into the trees.

The amenities appropriate to the occasion were observed, the seconds asking both parties if they could not come to terms without recourse to pistol fire. Dujarier took the opportunity to explain that he had been under the influence of wine at the party and that his insults had not been deliberate. He was willing to offer an apology if his opponent would accept it.

Beauvallon, bent on revenge, refused. He chose to believe that Dujarier was trying to persecute him and his relatives, and he intended to call a halt for all time to this practice. His words, as well as his manner, indicated his intent to shoot to kill.

The seconds for both principals hastened to remind him that under the dueling code the token spilling of blood was sufficient to satisfy honor. Beauvallon listened to them but made no reply.

The seconds made a minute inspection of both weapons, then gave Beauvallon his choice. He spent more than five minutes weighing and balancing both pistols while the shivering Dujarier waited. Beauvallon made his selection, and the pistols were duly loaded.

The seconds measured the clearing and placed their respective principals. It was now 10:35 A.M., more than an hour and a half after the duel had been scheduled to take place.

The chief seconds simultaneously gave the word, "You may fire at will!"

Dujarier took aim and fired. His shot went wild, and he dropped his pistol to the snow-covered ground.

Beauvallon smiled, then took so much time aiming his weapon that Dumas called out to him in a hoarse voice not to prolong the agony.

Dujarier stood absolutely still facing his opponent, proving—if such proof was necessary—that he was a man of courage.

Beauvallon's bullet entered his opponent's face near the bridge of his nose, producing a concussion of the spine.

Dr. de Guise rushed forward, knowing the wound was mortal.

Miraculously Dujarier stood erect for another moment or two before collapsing in the physician's arms. Dr. de Guise pronounced him dead.

Beauvallon bowed to Dumas, the doctor, and the seconds, then returned to his carriage.

Dumas went straight to Dujarier's apartment, where he found Lola Montez near frenzy. Much later he wrote that he had spent the entire drive trying to compose the statement he would make to her, but words proved unnecessary. Lola took one long look at his face, screamed, and then fainted. The physician summoned by Dumas administered laudanum as a sedative.

Still in a state of shock two days later, Lola was unable to attend the funeral. Four of the pallbearers—Dumas, Balzac, Mery, and Girardin—paid a formal call on her at Dujarier's apartment to offer their condolences. Her lover's mother had come to Paris from her home in the country, and there was talk of arranging a meeting between the two women. But neither woman was well enough, and the idea was abandoned.

Meantime the police opened an investigation of the duel. Beauvallon's tardiness in making his appearance in the Bois required an explanation, and it was also rumored that his pistol had been loaded with an iron ball much heavier than that ordinarily used in affairs of honor. Beauvallon was not available for questioning—he had found it expedient to slip across the Spanish border, accompanied by his principal second.

Dujarier's death was a blow from which Lola did not recover for a long time. In later years she told a few close friends that he was the only man in her life whom she truly loved.

Her immediate problem, as she began to regain her equilibrium, was lack of funds. Dujarier had been supporting her, but no additional money was available at the moment. Although he had left her the bulk of his estate, the courts would have to approve his will—a legal process that might require months to settle.

And so, although she had no heart for her work, Lola continued to rehearse for *La Biche au bois.* In the past she had always compensated for her lack of ability by giving a fiery, energetic performance. Now, however, her state of mind resulted in work so dismal that her colleagues shuddered as they watched her in rehearsals. *La Biche au bois* opened on April 12, one month after Dujarier's death, and although the musical comedy was a hit, Lola contributed nothing to its success. The opening night audience hissed her performance; she responded by thumbing her nose, a gesture that evoked catcalls.

The management of the Porte-Saint-Martin did not replace her, perhaps because they knew the audiences enjoyed heckling her, and she played the entire engagement, performing three nights each week from April until the end of September. There was little or no improvement in her performances, and the baiting of Lola Montez became a nightly treat for the audience. She kept her temper in check, but it was as obvious to her as it was to the theatrical community that her career on the Paris stage would come to an end when *La Biche au bois* closed.

While Dujarier's will was awaiting the pleasure of the courts, Lola remained in France. Dumas, who felt considerable sympathy for Lola, said in letters written at the time that she had nowhere else to go.

Beauvallon had returned to France upon learning that no legal action had been taken against his seconds, and believing that the duel had been forgotten by the authorities. He was mistaken; the police worked slowly, and the due process of law was even slower. By the beginning of July, 1845, the King's Procurator was ready to act, and Beauvallon was formally charged with the murder of Dujarier. The prosecution insisted that the atmosphere in Paris would become too heated if the trial were held there, and the case was assigned to the Assize Court of Rouen.

The appearance of Lola Montez and Alexandre Dumas, summoned as witnesses for the prosecution, would guarantee a crowded courtroom. Attorneys for Beauvallon obtained postponement after postponement as they tried in vain to have the trial shifted back to Paris, and during these months Lola's living expenses were paid by the Crown. This was fortunate, as she had no need to dip into the funds she had saved from her theatrical engagement.

The trial opened in mid-March of 1846, a year after Dujarier's death. Alexandre Dumas spent a full three days on the witness stand, to the delight of the spectators who occupied every seat in the Rouen courtroom. The courtesans who had attended the supper party at which Dujarier and Beauvallon had exchanged harsh words were also called, and these gaudily attired young women, who contributed little of substance to the case, further titillated the provincial audience and helped set the scene for the prosecution's star witness.

Lola Montez appeared in one of her close-fitting black gowns, a black veil over her face and a fringed black shawl over her shoulders. The year of mourning for Dujarier had passed, so her attire was inappropriate, but her entrance created a sensation in the courtroom. Then, removing her veil with a sweeping gesture, she gave one of her more inspired performances.

Her story began quietly. She had been worried about Dujarier but had relaxed when he lied to her about the identity of his opponent. Had she known that Beauvallon, an expert shot, was to be his foe, she would have gone to the police in order to prevent the duel.

Soon she was weeping, and even the presiding judge was seen to wipe his eyes and blow his nose. Lola ended her statement on a dramatic note: "If everything else had failed," she was quoted by the Paris newspapers, "I would have gone to the rendezvous myself."

That was the only portion of her testimony the attorneys for the defense chose to question in their cross-examination. Why, they asked, would Mlle. Montez have elected to witness the duel?

"Witness it?" Lola cried. "I would have taken Dujarier's place! I would have insisted upon it! I am familiar with firearms, gentlemen, and had I taken aim at the assassin Beauvallon, I assure you *I* would not have missed my target!"

The pandemonium in the courtroom was so great that the presiding judge ordered a thirty-minute adjournment.

Beauvallon was acquitted of the murder charge, but did not escape without being penalized. He was ordered to pay damages of 20,000 gold francs to Dujarier's mother, and another 10,000 in gold to the dead man's sister. Lola Montez, who had no legal standing as Dujarier's betrothed, was awarded nothing.

Some of the Paris gossip columnists who attended the trial noted in print that Dujarier's mother did not speak to the young foreigner her son had intended to marry and that Dujarier's sister followed her mother's example. Lola, it appeared, was not acceptable by the standards of provincial ladies of stature, and it is significant that neither in her *Autobiography* nor elsewhere does Lola mention the snub.

The disposition of Dujarier's estate had been held in abeyance until the murder trial was concluded, and when Lola returned to Paris from Rouen, she expected the courts to approve the will that Dujarier had written the night before his death. Upon her arrival she found a letter asking her to get in touch with a prominent lawyer. She went to see him, and was informed that he represented Mme. Dujarier, who was planning to contest her son's will. She was further informed that Dujarier's half-interest in *La Presse,* his real estate holdings, and his cash and securities—together worth more than half a million francs—rightly belonged to Mme. Dujarier and her daughter.

Lola was stunned, but she recovered immediately. She told the lawyer she would fight.

Her response was not unexpected, and the lawyer presumed to offer her some advice. She and Dujarier had been living on the permissive fringe of French society, he said, but France was essentially a conservative nation, in which the courts of law constituted one of the most conservative elements. Dujarier had inherited the better part of his fortune from his late father, and the courts would favor the substitution of his previous will, in which he had left everything to his beloved mother and sister. No judge would want to open himself to the criticism of his peers by awarding such a large sum to a foreign dancer who called herself Spanish but obviously was of some other nationality and who had so little regard for moral propriety that she had lived openly with Dujarier in the months prior to his death. A mistress was expected to get what she could from her lover while he was alive.

However, the lawyer concluded, Mme. Dujarier was not insensitive to the plight of the young woman. Because her son had made it plain that he was fond of Lola, Mme. Dujarier was willing to give her the sum of 50,000 francs. In return Lola would be expected to drop the case.

Unwilling to give a quick answer, Lola sought the help of

Dujarier's friends. Émile de Girardin, who could hardly have relished the prospect of becoming business partner to an adventuress, urged her to accept the offer. So did Dumas, who had her interests at heart. Madame Dujarier's lawyer had spoken the truth, he said. No French court would uphold Lola's claim, and her lover's final will undoubtedly would be invalidated.

Some of the more sensational Paris newspapers began speculating in print as to what decision Lola would make. One or two said she would fight for justice and take her chances in court, but the rest predicted that she would accept Mme. Dujarier's offer.

There were no libel laws worthy of the name in mid-nineteenth-century France, and it was the custom of the press to say what it pleased, quoting or misquoting individuals at will when such quotes made a better story. It is therefore difficult to judge the accuracy of a quote that appeared in the *Globe*. The anonymous author of an alleged interview with Lola Montez wrote that she had told him, "The moment I get a nice, round lump sum of money in hand, I am going to try to hook a prince."

Lola may well have made the statement, as prophetic as it was provocative. It seems unlikely, however, that she would have confided in a journalist for the penny press or that she would have described her ambitions in such crude terms.

She did accept Mme. Dujarier's offer. Then new complications developed. The old lady apparently decided she had been too generous, and Lola received only half the promised sum. This was too much—she hired an attorney of her own and filed suit for damages, demanding a sum of 100,000 francs in addition to the 25,000 still owed to her.

Mme. Dujarier realized she had gone too far, and made an out-of-court settlement: Lola was paid the additional 25,000 gold francs and an additional 50,000 as balm for her injured dignity. Although the sum did not make her wealthy, it gave her greater financial independence than she had ever enjoyed, and she made her plans accordingly.

Her career in Paris was ended, and the only life open to her there was that of a courtesan. She stayed in the city only long enough to have a dazzling new wardrobe made. On her last night in Paris, she dined with Alexandre Dumas, but was vague when questioned about her future plans.

According to her *Autobiography*, she dressed in black and went the next morning at dawn to the cemetery where Dujarier was buried. She placed a single white rose on his grave; she wept. "Farewell, my love," she said, and without further ado left Paris, presumably for all time.

[CHAPTER IX]

When Lola left Paris in the spring of 1846, at the age of twenty-eight, it was no longer possible for her to live and travel in comfortable anonymity. She sought attention, to be sure, but there must have been times in the months that followed her departure when she wished she were less of a public figure. More than a year had passed since the death of Dujarier, and by now she had readjusted her sights and established new goals.

These goals were clear to anyone who cared to read about her in the Paris newspapers, which kept their readers informed of her movements. Lola was man-hunting; setting her glamour traps at the watering resorts favored by the blue-bloods and their peers in the newly developing aristocracy, the middle-class industrialists whose factories and plants had made them enormously wealthy. Her leather traveling boxes filled with new clothes and her purse with gold francs, the adventuress was on the prowl.

She traveled southeast. Her first stop was in Savoy at Aix-les-Bains, the health resort whose thermal springs had soothed the weary and rejuvenated the crotchety since Roman times. After a few days there, Lola became restless. The strong sulfur odors made her sneeze. What was worse, she discovered that the other guests were, without exception, elderly gentlemen accompanied by their equally elderly wives.

Her next stop was Wiesbaden, across the German border.

Finding things no better there, she left for the most popular of resorts, Baden-Baden, where the clientele was so aristocratic that Balzac had been refused a hotel room on his first visit to the spa. It was in Baden-Baden that she made her first royal conquest.

Prince Heinrich LXXII was the undisputed ruler of the principality of Reuss, a domain so small it could be crossed in three hours by someone riding a horse at a canter. His Catholic Highness was an elderly widower whose farmlands in a number of German states earned him a large income. Heinrich's penchant for attractive young women was well known, as was the fact that none of his affairs lasted for very long, although no one quite knew why.

Lola took aim. Within a few days of her arrival at Baden-Baden, she was presented to Heinrich. He had seen Lola—who had a lifelong aversion to aimless strolls—walking on the lawn only a few yards from the windows of his ground-floor hotel suite.

As the friendship developed, the Paris *Globe* did not fail to remind its readers of Lola's prophetic comment on the subject in these same columns. His Highness had invited Mlle. Montez to visit him in Reuss, said the *Globe*, and she had been pleased to accept.

The royal domicile was a damp, gloomy castle built in the twelfth century, and neither Heinrich nor any of his ancestors had found it necessary to modernize the place. The etiquette of the court was stifling, the ruler apparently demanding formality to compensate for the lack of breathing space in his tiny realm. Lola was given her own suite, but the nights were so cold that she had to purchase blankets and bedding in order to keep warm. Finding the meals at the royal table inedible, she was told by a majordomo that most guests preferred to pay for their food, which was purchased for them. Lola was indignant, but she was also hungry. She paid.

Her meetings with Heinrich were infrequent. They usually took place in the drafty great hall of the castle, where the old man sat on his faded throne, surrounded by courtiers. It quickly became apparent to Lola that Heinrich was not interested in having an affair with her but was enjoying the international stir her presence created. She was offered the use of the royal stable, but was told there were no saddles suitable for her. She was so bored that she paid the chief groom out of her own purse for the ladies' saddle he bought on her behalf.

One afternoon when Lola had nothing better to do, she inadvertently walked through a newly seeded flower bed on the castle grounds. Heinrich, who happened to see her, was so incensed that he banished her from the principality, writing her expulsion order himself. Other royal mistresses, Lola knew, had been dismissed on equally flimsy charges.

This one, however, was made of sterner stuff. She refused to leave until Heinrich repaid her in gold for the expenses she had incurred. She presented him with a carefully detailed list, which she had had the foresight to pad. His Highness swore that he had never been subjected to such an insult and would not give her a copper. Lola informed him that if he did not pay, she would inform the world that he was an impotent old man who used pretty girls as window dressing.

Heinrich capitulated, giving her the sum she had demanded, and then enjoyed the last, petty laugh. Lola's belongings were taken to the border by a small train of donkey carts, but she was provided with no transportation. The spring day was pleasant, and Lola enjoyed her walk through the fields, arriving at the frontier before sundown.

There she was forced to make a choice. To the north lay Prussia, which she knew sufficiently well to avoid. Only a few miles to the east stood an estate where Franz Liszt was living with his latest mistress, a German princess, and Lola had no desire to see Liszt again. She would be retracing her steps if she traveled to the west. That left the kingdom of Bavaria, the wealthiest of the German states, which lay to the south. Despite all that was written about Lola Montez' decision to visit Bavaria, there is no real evidence to indicate that she went there to ensnare the King. On the contrary, her choice seems to have been more or less accidental.

Of all the German states, Bavaria was exceeded in size only by Prussia. Its rich farms and forests spread over some 30,000 square miles, and its position in the Danube River basin made it a natural trade center. In the mid-1840's Bavaria had a population of about 4 million, more than 50,000 of whom lived in the capital and principal city, Munich.

The Bavarians, proud of their long heritage of independence and cultural advancement, regarded the other German kingdoms and principalities as barbarian lands. They looked to Vienna, the German-speaking capital of the Austro-Hungarian empire, for much of their intellectual and artistic inspiration, and they were proud of their own accomplishments in architecture, the theater, and music. Their universities were among the oldest and most distinguished in the German states, and a number of them enjoyed international reputations.

More than 80 percent of the people of Bavaria were Roman Catholics, and the country was regarded at the time as one of the most politically conservative in Europe. But the surface was deceptive. When Lola Montez arrived in the late spring of 1846, the revolutions of 1848 that would sweep the Continent were less than two years distant, and there was already a ferment of discontent in Bavaria, as elsewhere.

Partly responsible were the economic pressures caused by the Industrial Revolution. Manufacturing plants sprang up in Munich, Nuremberg, Augsburg, and other cities; there, men and women worked under wretched conditions, while the owners grew wealthier. Some of the more prominent universities were administered by the Jesuits, who were in the forefront of the reform movement in Bavaria as in other lands, and a strong spirit of radicalism pervaded the student corps. Even the more conservative elements were dissatisfied with their political lot: in other countries the people were speaking in voices that became louder each year, but the Bavarians were ruled as they had been for centuries—by a monarch and a small group of nobles who paid lip service to the democratic spirit now rising throughout Europe but who continued to rule as they pleased with the aid of a secret-police service that knew little and cared less about so-called civil liberties.

The ancient traditions had been reversed—for a time—early in the century. King Maximilian I had established a parliament on the British model after the fall of Napoleon gave him effective control of his country, and for a decade, until his death in 1825, he had ruled as a constitutional monarch.

His son Ludwig I had tried to follow Maximilian's example, but Parliament opposed his expensive building program, his demands for huge sums of money to buy works of art, and his efforts to encourage the growth of art in the country. An unsuccessful revolution in 1831 had soured him on the principles of democracy, and over the last decade and a half Ludwig had become increasingly authoritarian. With his encouragement a party known as the Ultramontaines had come to power in 1837, and the head of that party, Karl von Abel, became Prime Minister. Ludwig and Abel now ruled together, Abel always acting with the King's consent and in his name.

After the revolution of 1831, the Jesuits had gained increasing power, the younger members of the order becoming the administrators of the universities, while their elders became active in affairs of government. Ludwig, easily swayed by men of power, issued a royal decree that made Catholicism the state religion, and Protestants were forbidden to practice their faith in public. Ludwig, Abel, and the older Jesuits tolerated no opposition, and a tight censorship prevented freedom of expression.

Ludwig, sixty-one years old when Lola Montez entered his realm and his life, was an exceptionally complicated man. He had been born in France, where King Louis XVI had become his godfather, and he had been taught by French tutors to respect all things related to the Bourbon line of kings. He had been dismayed by the rise of Napoleon, and by his father's treaty of alliance with the great French Emperor.

A devout Catholic, young Ludwig became uneasy as he watched the spread of Protestantism. A natural liking for conspiracy led him to join in a plot against the life of Napoleon, but his father learned of it in time and sent him off to Italy to study and keep out of mischief. In Milan, Florence, and other Italian cities, Ludwig acquired his great love of Renaissance paintings and sculpture.

At the request of Napoleon, who knew nothing about the young man's participation in a plot against him, Ludwig was called home and given command of a division. He fought with surprising distinction, considering that he sympathized with the Emperor's foes. After the fall of Napoleon in 1815, he returned to Italy and spent nearly two years in Rome, later proclaiming them the happiest of his life.

Recalled to Munich by his father, he spent the better part of a decade in preparation for his role as Elector, or King, and succeeded to the throne in his fortieth year. Art remained his abiding passion, and he poured funds into the creation of a new Munich, a city that would rival Florence. To his credit he almost succeeded.

Although Ludwig left the affairs of state that did not interest him to his Prime Minister and the other cabinet officers, he was no dilettante. Museums, churches, and triumphal arches cost large sums of money, and his running battle with Parliament in the early years of his reign left such a lasting impression on him that he constituted himself the principal guardian of the royal treasury. He allowed no one else to approve state expenditures, and no monies were paid out of the treasury without his personal authorization.

Ludwig became more miserly with each passing year; he drove his ministers to despair. When the army purchased some new cannon without his approval, he refused to pay the foundry in Prussia for the merchandise and forced the generals who had been responsible to foot the bill themselves. He questioned the cost of a dinner party at a Bavarian legation abroad; he even refused to permit the purchase of some $10,000 worth of new textbooks for students at the university, although the school was a special source of pride to him. "I read secondhand books when I was a student," he said, "and I am the Elector. Surely commoners do not require expensive new books."

The twists of Ludwig's paradoxical nature were endless. He was as fluent in French, Italian, and English as he was in German, but his pan-Germanism became so pronounced that he issued a decree in 1840 forbidding the use of any other language at his court, and personally sent into exile any subject who spoke a tongue other than German in his presence. He was strongly, sometimes violently anti-Semitic, yet he offered financial and personal help to a number of young Jewish writers, composers, and painters. He lived in the midst of priceless art treasures, but he wore old suits of clothes until they were threadbare. He built canals, encouraged industry by investing his own money in new plants, and sought improved methods of agriculture, yet he would not allow the expenditure of state funds for any of these purposes.

He was equally inconsistent and unpredictable in his private life. In his twenties he had had the good fortune to fall in love with a girl whose high birth entitled her to share his lofty station in life. According to no less an authority on the subject than Napoleon Bonaparte, Princess Theresa of Saxe-Hildburghausen was the most beautiful and accomplished young princess in Europe. She spoke several languages, played the piano with the skill of a professional musician, and was an accomplished still-life painter. She was widely read, and so delighted her father-in-law with her wit that, after the death of his queen, she became the official hostess at all court receptions and dinners.

Theresa was firm in her loyalties to her husband in spite of his idiosyncrasies, and she bore him seven healthy children, all of whom were educated under his direct supervision. She was liberal in her views, and when Ludwig's policies became increasingly repressive, she used her influence for the first time in an attempt to modify his harsh decrees.

The Queen made these efforts soon after the birth of her last child, and it is possible that Ludwig's resentment over her interference was responsible for his sudden change in attitude toward her. Until that time he had never been unfaithful to her and had consistently praised her as a model of all that was good in a woman. Overnight, however, he announced to his intimates that she had acquired the drabness of the middle-class German housewife, and he made it plain in public as well as in private that she bored him.

Soon afterward Queen Theresa moved to her own quarters in another wing of the royal palace in Munich, and every summer she went off on holiday trips accompanied only by some of her children and her ladies-in-waiting. Meanwhile Ludwig took a succession of mistresses, most of them actresses of no account who spent a few weeks or months in a small palace suite conveniently located near the King's bedchamber before being sent on their way with their memories and a trinket or two as a token.

Ludwig's flagrant infidelities were common knowledge, but Queen Theresa permitted no mention of his affairs in her presence and would allow no one to malign Ludwig in conversation with her. As nearly as anyone could tell, she was still in love with him, and neither her children nor her closest friends ever heard her speak ill of him. She knew, of course, that his romances were not serious, and that he took only a passing interest in the pretty, vapid girls who moved in and out of his bedchamber.

That situation changed drastically in the early autumn of 1846 when a far more aggressive and intelligent young beauty called herself to King Ludwig's attention.

[CHAPTER X]

Lola Montez' involvement with Ludwig I of Bavaria—who, thanks to his relationship with her, would go down in books as "Mad King Ludwig"—changed the course of European history. Perhaps the most curious aspect of this most notorious of nineteenth-century liaisons was the vehemence with which both principals consistently denied it. Ludwig swore on oath to the Archbishop of Munich that Lola had never been his mistress. In her *Autobiography* Lola insisted that she and the King had been friends, nothing more, and she stuck to this story to her dying day. There is only one logical explanation: the upheavals caused by the affair were so great and so far-reaching that both Ludwig and Lola must have been ashamed to admit to the world that their illicit relationship could have been responsible.

The facts of the century's most publicized affair, virtually all of them documented, speak for themselves. Certainly the dramatic high point of Lola Montez' life began on a low note. She arrived in Munich late in the spring of 1846, unheralded and unnoticed, and for several dreary months lived there in almost complete anonymity.

Through no fault of her own, she had arrived at the wrong season. The weather was warmer than usual, and Queen Theresa had already gone off to a watering resort with several of her younger children. King Ludwig had transferred his capital to one of his summer palaces in the Alps, accompanied by the Prime Minister and most of the key members of his government. Overnight Munich became a provincial city.

Bavarians took great pride in their theaters, and Munich boasted more playhouses than any other German city. Foremost among these was the Court Theatre, which presented plays by native Bavarian authors as well as those of the great Viennese playwrights. The fare was varied. Approximately one-third of each season was devoted to light opera, which catered to the Bavarians' fondness for music. The Court's standards were high, and the theater had developed an international reputation.

Lola knew that an appearance at the Court would launch her in the circles where she wanted to become known; as soon as she established herself in a small apartment, she went to the theater seeking employment. There she learned that the Court was closing for the summer, and she was asked to return early in the autumn, when casting would begin for the following year.

A few of the lesser theaters remained open, and Lola might have found work at one of them. Instead she decided to wait for the reopening of the Court. Convinced that nowhere else could she attain the professional and social standing she sought, she voluntarily condemned herself to a summer of inactivity.

The quiet was even greater than she had anticipated. Members of the diplomatic corps and most of the high-ranking aristocrats had followed Ludwig to the Bavarian Alps, and the only people of means left in the city were the hard-working, middle-class factory and plant owners. Many of these men would have been delighted to entertain a spectacularly endowed young woman, but experience had taught Lola that reputation was a precious asset, and she behaved accordingly.

She went sight-seeing; she improved her ability to read, write, and speak German; and above all, as she sat in cafés and parks, she listened to the gossip of the people. It was impossible to learn much about the true state of affairs in the country from the rigidly censored newspapers, but people talked, and Lola had a sharp ear.

Ludwig I, she learned, was the ultimate authority in her new country. Parliament had been shorn of its power, and the government ministers followed the King's wishes, establishing policies of their own only in those fields in which he had little or no interest. The senior Jesuits also served Ludwig's pleasure, their authority stemming exclusively from him.

What Lola heard about Ludwig's personal life was much more fascinating. People whispered that he had been accompanied to his retreat in the Alps by a young blonde singer from Vienna; that she had departed within a fortnight; that she had been replaced by an unknown actress from Saxony. It was a standing joke that the actress would no longer be a member of the royal household by the time Ludwig returned to Munich in the autumn. The implications were obvious: it might be possible for an ambitious and clever young woman to call herself to Ludwig's attention and thereby make good the boast, real or concocted, that had been attributed to her in the Paris *Globe*.

The summer was the most uneventful period that Lola had known in years, but she had plenty of money and, apparently, a degree of patience that was uncharacteristic. Her future was bright, even if she alone knew it.

Early in September, when the first frost appeared on the grounds of his summer palace in the Alps, Ludwig and his court returned to Munich. They were followed a few days later by Queen Theresa and the royal children. Soon afterward the Parliament reopened, and the King, accompanied by his wife, drove through the streets in an open carriage to address the "representatives of the people." The ceremony, one of the most colorful annual events in the country, was celebrated in true German style with marching bands and a parade of infantry, cavalry, and artillery. Also participating were the nobles, the trade-guild representatives, and the university students who belonged to various undergraduate fraternal organizations. Even the archbishop took part, bestowing his blessing on the crowds that lined the parade route, and the senior Jesuits made a rare public appearance, watching from a reviewing stand.

Virtually the entire population of the city turned out for the event, and one of the most interested spectators was Lola Montez. Many years later she recorded her impression of King Ludwig as he appeared to her that day:

The Elector's eye was so bright and his expression so keen that he did not look like a man of more than sixty years. His was the most modest uniform to be seen in the parade, and beneath it was a body accustomed to regular exercise. He sat erect in his coach, waving, smiling, and sometimes calling out greetings to the many he knew by name in the great crowd; it was plain to all that his subjects loved him, and that he returned their affection.

She entertained no fond memories of Theresa, however. Even the passage of years did not soften her scorn for the Queen:

The Elector's consort was withdrawn, a tight smile was frozen on her lips, and she did not try to contain her transparent belief that the people were far beneath her. Scarcely aware of the tumult accorded her royal husband by his loyal subjects, the elderly, ailing lady looked as though she wished she were elsewhere.

With the return of the King and the opening of Parliament, Munich came to life again. Within a day or two the Court Theatre opened its doors to audition players who wanted to appear in the coming season's repertory. Lola was one of the first to arrive. The Court's directors, who read the Paris critics and were aware of her debacle there, did not appear to be impressed. They consented to give her an audition, however, and when she danced for them, her performance confirmed their worst fears. There was no place for amateurs or even semiprofessionals in the Court Theatre company, and Lola was gently but very firmly rejected.

A woman less determined and ambitious might have changed her plans, but Lola, who had more or less expected a refusal, was ready with a substitute scheme. During the long summer she had made it her business to learn something about the personalities and habits of various members of the royal household, and had already made up her mind to concentrate on Ludwig's personal aide-de-camp, Count Otto von Rechberg.

A bachelor of about forty, the Count shared his royal master's enthusiasm for lovely young women and was reportedly even more of a connoisseur than Ludwig. The rest was easy for the most striking beauty ever to visit Munich.

Count von Rechberg kept his own apartment a short distance from the palace, and it was his custom to stop off every morning on his way to work at a café that overlooked the spacious palace gardens. Lola waited until a bright, clear morning when she felt reasonably sure the Count would be drinking his coffee and eating his breakfast sausage roll out of doors. Mounting a rented horse, she went for a canter, and allowed herself to be thrown from the saddle directly in front of the café. The performance was one of her best: she landed at Rechberg's feet.

The Count was enchanted. Lola graciously allowed him to buy her a cup of coffee, and they struck up a friendship. Whether she allowed the friendship to develop into an affair or just hinted at the delights in store for him if he helped her is not known. Lola maintained a lifelong discreet silence on the subject, and Rechberg, in the light of later developments, was reluctant to admit he had ever exchanged so much as a word with her.

However she may have managed it, Lola persuaded Count von Rechberg to present her to Ludwig. Only the King himself had the power, she pointed out, to insist that the management of the Court Theatre hire her for an engagement. Presumably Ludwig had more important matters to occupy his time and thoughts, but in itself the request was harmless enough, and when Lola was persuasive, few men could resist her. Rechberg agreed.

On October 8, 1846, at three o'clock in the afternoon, Lola presented herself at the palace and announced that she had an appointment with the royal aide-de-camp. The engagement was confirmed, and the sentries escorted the young woman in the tight-fitting black velvet gown through the long palace corridors.

Rechberg awaited Lola in an anteroom adjoining the royal study, where King Ludwig was signing the first of the bills passed by his rubber-stamp Parliament. The aide went inside to seek an audience for the "Spanish dancer." The door was ajar, and Lola could hear the King refusing to interrupt his work for a favor-seeking stranger. The Count made a feeble attempt to persuade him to change his mind; Ludwig would not.

Assuming this proximity to the throne of Bavaria to be a unique opportunity, Lola acted accordingly. Brushing aside the two startled sentries who stood on guard outside the study, she entered the royal presence.

The meeting of Ludwig and the woman with whom his name would be linked for all time was at least half as sensational as later accounts reported it to be. The facts were subsequently authenticated by Count von Rechberg; by one Lieutenant Hoffman, who was acting as captain of the royal guard; and by Ludwig himself, although none of these gentlemen ever offered an explanation for what happened. Lola herself, questioned by interviewers for the rest of her life, refused to discuss the matter, and in her *Autobiography* kept demurely silent.

In a word, Lola Montez made her initial appearance before the King of Bavaria with all or a portion of her breasts on display. The cause of this extraordinary circumstance has been the topic of speculation for a hundred and twenty-five years. The most widely accepted theory has never been verified: one of the sentries, reaching out in an attempt to bar Lola's impetuous entry, succeeded only in grasping the fabric of her gown, which ripped as she raced past him.

Another version has it that Lola deliberately bared her breasts as she came into the study, knowing that Ludwig would be unable to dismiss her after viewing these wonders. A popular variation of this account suggested that the sentry ripped Lola's dress slightly, whereupon she seized her opportunity and completed the damage herself. The most dramatic version has Lola grabbing Ludwig's sword and using it to slash her gown, but this is nonsense. Ludwig would hardly have been wearing a sword while at work in his study, but even if he had been, it would have been a dress sword with a blunt cutting edge.

However the accident—if it was an accident—took place, it did occur. Ludwig, his aide-de-camp, and the captain of the guard made no mention of the King's immediate reaction, which must be left to the imagination of the reader. All three sources agreed that for a long moment no one moved, and that Ludwig himself was the first to recover. He picked up a short cloak from a chair and threw it over the shoulders of the intruder.

By that time Lola had won her battle, inadvertently or otherwise, and was granted the audience she sought. She encountered no difficulties, and Ludwig's intervention with the management of the Court Theatre brought prompt results. Fifty-five hours later, on the evening of October 19, Spanish dancer Lola Montez made her Bavarian debut on the stage of the Court Theatre, appearing between the first and second acts of an operetta with a title that was absurdly appropriate, *The Enchanted Prince.*

Nearly a half-century later, in 1894, the Countess Louise von Kobell described that occasion in her book, *Unter den vier ersten Königen Bayerns:*

> On the 9th October, 1846, as I was going down Briennerstrasse, near the Bayersdorf Palace, I saw approaching me a lady, gowned in black, with a veil thrown over her head, and a fan in her hand. Suddenly something seemed to flash across my vision, and I stood stock still, gazing into the eyes that had dazzled me. They shone upon me from a pale countenance, which assumed a laughing expression before my bewildered stare. Then she went, or rather swept on, past me. I forgot all of my governess' injunctions against looking around, and stood staring after her, until she disappeared from view. Like her, I told myself, must have been the fairies in the nursery tales. I returned home breathless, and told them of my adventure. "That," said my father grimly, "must have been the Spanish dancer, Lola Montez." I went to the Court Theatre on Saturday, the 10th October; I came much too early to my seat, and read full of eagerness the announcement: "*Der verwünschene Prinz,* a play with music in three acts, by J. von Plotz. During the *entr'actes,* Mademoiselle Lola Montez of Madrid will appear in her Spanish national dances."
>
> Full of impatience I saw the curtain rise, sat through the first act and saw the curtain fall again. Now it rose once more, and I saw my fairy of yesterday—Lola Montez.
>
> In the pit, they clapped and hissed; the last, explained my neighbor, because of the rumors abroad that Lola was an emissary of the English Freemasons, an enemy of the Jesuits—a coquette,

too, who had had amorous adventures in all parts of the world, according to the newspapers.

Lola Montez took the center of the stage, clothed not in the usual tights and short skirts of the ballet girl, but in a Spanish costume of silk and lace, with here and there a glittering diamond. Fire seemed to shoot from her wonderful green-blue eyes, and she bowed like one of the Graces before the King, who occupied the royal box. Then she danced after the fashion of her country, swaying on her hips, and changing from one posture to another, each excelling the former in beauty.

While she danced she riveted the attention of all the spectators, their gaze followed the sinuous swayings of her body, in their expression now full of glowing passion, now of lightsome playfulness. Not until she ceased her rhythmic movements was the spell broken . . . On the 14th October, 1846, Lola Montez appeared for the second and last time at the Court Theatre. She danced the "Cachucha" in the comedy, *Der Weiberfeind von Benedix,* and danced the "Fandango" with Herr Opfermann in the *entr'acte* of the play, *Müller und Miller.* In order to drown any manifestations of displeasure, the pit was occupied by a claque of policemen in plain clothes, and by theatre attendants. The precaution was unnecessary, as Lola Montez exercised a charm that was universal. The King had received her in audience, as he was accustomed to receive foreign *artistes;* her beauty and her stimulating conversation captivated Ludwig I.

Frau von Kobell's account is accurate in all but a few details. It is true that Lola was hissed by the Court Theatre audience in the presence of the King on October 10, but at that time it had not yet been rumored that she was a secret agent of the English Freemasons who had come to Bavaria in order to drive the Jesuits out of power. That story did not spread until she had established her influence over Ludwig and become the single most important force in the country.

She was hissed for the simple reason that her performance was too frightful to be tolerated by a discerning audience—not even the presence of the King could keep the patrons of the Court Theatre from expressing their displeasure over the amateur gyrations on the stage. Only a child as young as Louise von Kobell could have found the performance enjoyable.

It is also true that members of the secret police were present on the occasion of Lola's second and final appearance at the Court Theatre four days later. By then the King was eager to further her career, and it was easy enough for him to order the police to prohibit demonstrations against the enchantress.

Frau von Kobell failed to mention the reason why Lola's theatrical career in Bavaria was terminated so abruptly. Not even the might and majesty of the King could persuade the directors of the theater to hire the dancer again. They knew, as did everyone else who saw Lola's performance, that the great Court Theatre would become the laughingstock of Europe if they permitted her to grace their stage again. The "Spanish Dancer" was, nonetheless, paid a staggering sum for her two appearances—so staggering, in fact, that we can only assume the salary to have been privately paid out of the royal purse.

It is the first instance on record, but far from the last, that Ludwig, known throughout the Continent as a miser, poured riches into the delicate, grasping hands of Lola Montez.

Certainly Frau von Kobell did not exaggerate when she wrote that Ludwig had been captivated by Lola. Her conquest, far greater than even she had dreamed, would spark a revolution, topple a throne, and threaten the governments of half the nations in Europe.

[CHAPTER XI]

Prime Minister Abel of Bavaria recounted in his memoirs a scene that took place in the royal quarters of King Ludwig's palace on October 15, 1846, a week after Lola Montez had called herself to the attention of the monarch. The Prime Minister was trying to describe to Ludwig a power struggle in Parliament, the intricacies of which Ludwig would ordinarily have been quick to grasp. On this occasion, however, the royal mind wandered repeatedly, until Abel finally reprimanded the King.

Ludwig apologized, then added, "I know not how or why, but I am bewitched."

Soon the tongues of all Europe were wagging: Ludwig obviously was proving the truth of the adage about an old fool. The gossip about the King and Lola was reported everywhere. Young Benjamin Disraeli, sick in a London bed with an attack of influenza, wrote a long letter on the subject to his sister. A scurrilous poem about Ludwig and Lola that was passed from hand to hand at the imperial court in St. Petersburg was repressed because the Tsar's secret police believed an attack on any monarch to be an assault on the institution of monarchy. And a Bavarian expatriate, a former member of Ludwig's household staff who was traveling in the American West, sent a letter to a friend on the eastern seaboard in which he explained that the King's action in no way surprised him. Ludwig, he said, worshiped artistic perfection, and if the accounts of his new mistress were accurate, she was the most beautiful of living women.

Ludwig's biographers and other students of the period subsequently agreed with this analysis. For many years attractive young women had provided the King with the necessary biological outlets. He had, however, always reserved his emotional enthusiasms for masterworks of painting and sculpture, for which he had been willing to pay any price. These works of art were housed in a palace gallery known as *Die Schönheitengalerie* and each week he held a reception there, at which commoners who appreciated art mingled with government officials, high-ranking aristocrats, and members of the diplomatic corps.

On October 18 the King's guests were startled when he appeared at the reception with Lola Montez on his arm. The actresses with whom he had consorted in the past had been carefully hidden away in private palace suites, under no circumstances appearing with him in public. But Ludwig was proud to show off Lola—as though he had added another priceless treasure to his collection of art works.

It soon became evident to Ludwig-watchers, a group that included everyone in a position of authority and most Bavarian commoners, that he was not involved in another of his inconsequential little romances. His relationship with Lola was different, and obviously special. Lola visited the palace only to attend the receptions in the art gallery, and on these occasions she and the King were never alone. Knowing there would be gossip, they were arranging their lives in a way that, they thought, would keep whispers to a minimum.

In this they were short-sighted and naïve. Lola moved out of her modest flat into a small but well-appointed villa on the Theresienstrasse, one of Munich's most fashionable boulevards. The house was purchased in her name, but the payment was made in gold, delivered in a burlap sack that bore the seal of the royal household treasury. This tidbit soon found its way into the newspapers of Paris and other foreign capitals.

According to the standards of the time the house was just

Then was I happy for feeling more deeply
What I possessed and what I lost;
It seemed that thy joy then went forever,
And that it could nevermore return.

Thou hast lost thy cheerfulness,
Persecution has robbed thee of it;
It has deprived thee of thy health,
The happiness of thy life is already departed.

But the firmer only, and more firmly
Thou hast tied me to thee;
Thou canst never draw me from thee—
Thou sufferest because thou lovest me.

In her *Autobiography* Lola tried to give the world a far different, more innocuous word portrait of her relationship with Ludwig. The attempt seems brazen, even for Lola—people everywhere knew that Ludwig had spent fortunes on her and that the powerful political, religious, and academic elements in Bavaria had become so incensed by Lola's interference in affairs of state that they had aroused the country against her. Ludwig, afraid for her life, and perhaps his own, had sent her away, but it had been too late to save himself—a revolution had forced him to escape into exile, too.

Every newspaper of consequence had reported on the subject in great detail. Hundreds of magazine articles had been written in a dozen languages, and books and plays on the drama appeared in London, Paris, Stockholm, and Amsterdam. Yet Lola continued to insist that the relationship was only platonic and political. She wrote:

The King manifested great surprise at some of the information I gave him about the struggle for power in France and was so deeply interested as to ask me to stay in Munich as his guest for a few days. I at first declined, and finally observed, "Will it not give cause for scandal against Your Majesty?" He said, "No, I have no fear of that." I consented to stay a few days, and renewed my conversation with the King several times on visits to him at his instance. These visits were ceremonious. I talked to the

King as I always do to everyone—truthfully, frankly and without concealment.

I told him of errors and abuses in his government, I told him of the perfidy of his ministers. Honest and unsuspecting, he did not believe it, but I proved it to him. I exposed to him especially the art, duplicity and villainy of his Prime Minister, Baron von Abel, a tool of the Jesuits who had wormed himself into his confidences. King Ludwig was convinced, in spite of all the scandalous fabrications that were circulated, that I was his friend, as I was most truly. For a long time his profligate and faithless counsellors could not imagine from whence their betrayed and abused master learned the facts as to their conduct. When they did, what a torrent of scandal and falsehood was opened upon me! I was everything that was bad and vile. But they could not injure me with the good King. Abel was determined to drive me away, and he plotted against me, raising all kinds of vile scandal about me, which he sent to France, Spain, England and the East Indies.

Lola's distortions of the truth were no worse in her descriptions of the fate she suffered in Bavaria than in other portions of her *Autobiography*. What makes them remarkable is not her denial of facts that had been verified but the highly political view she took of her role.

One wonders, certainly, why Lola dabbled in politics in the first place. The infatuated King had established her in a luxury she had never known. She had a large villa, servants to satisfy every whim, a growing bank account, and a collection of jewels worth perhaps half a million dollars. She had achieved an international fame far beyond that of any dancer and was recognized as a celebrity everywhere in the civilized world. Queen Victoria of England, who allegedly sniffed when Lola's name was mentioned in her presence, might join Queen Theresa of Bavaria in snubbing her, but Lola was indifferent to the opinions of "royal frumps," as she called them.

At thirty Lola had lifelong security, she was universally recognized as one of the great beauties of the age, and, if some people disapproved of her conduct, she had nevertheless made her name synonymous with glamour. By meddling in Bavarian affairs of state, by turning the King against his ministers, she placed her future in jeopardy, thereby defying every rule of self-preservation and common sense.

Why did she do it?

[CHAPTER XII]

In the years prior to the outbreak of the revolutions of 1848 throughout Europe, no man was more greatly feared in conservative Roman Catholic circles than Père Felicité Lamennais of France. A radical reformer determined to root out abuses of the Church from within, he had stirred up so much trouble that the Pope had denied him the right to exercise his functions as a priest. In no way discouraged, Father Lamennais had established his own philosophical circle in France, where he published a radical magazine, engaged in prolific correspondence with prominent persons, and goaded authority almost beyond endurance.

One of those who came under Lamennais' influence for a time was George Sand. She became his apostle, contributed articles to his publications and substantial sums of money to his cause until, like so many others, she quarreled and parted company with him. Lamennais was respected in French intellectual circles, even by those who disagreed with him, for the solidity of his philosophical thinking, and it was said that the younger, reform-minded Jesuits also thought highly of him. But there were few others anywhere in Europe who had a good word to say about him.

After the disastrous results of her sojourn in Bavaria, Lola claimed she had tried to help King Ludwig because she had been a close friend and disciple of Lamennais. This may well be the wildest of all her claims.

Lola could have met Lamennais in France, perhaps during the period she was living with Dujarier, but if their paths did cross, there is no record of a meeting. That she was a student of the dissident priest's philosophy is simply preposterous. Some readers may accept the assertion, often repeated by those who knew her, that Lola was uncommonly intelligent; but by no stretch of any imagination other than her own could she be considered a deep thinker. If she truly read the philosophy of Lamennais, it is the only time in her life she engaged in such an endeavor. At no time did she associate with anyone else of Lamennais' intellectual caliber, and no word she ever wrote or spoke for publication indicated that she had read the works of the priest.

Truth is better served by likening Lola's situation to that of a twentieth-century waitress catapulted to overnight fortune and fame as a motion-picture star. Lola's leap from modest means to great wealth was accomplished overnight, and her good fortune went to her head, warping her views and robbing her of whatever sense of proportion she had. She no sooner expressed a desire for something new than it was given to her, and when she exhausted her craving for material possessions, she developed a craving for actual power.

Her initial list of desires was seemingly endless. Although her villa was more than spacious enough for her needs, she added two new wings, one built of imported Italian marble and containing a reception hall where she could hold her own court. A lesser trifle she acquired was a bath carved out of a single block of cream-colored marble that was so high off the ground it required three steps to reach. Those steps were fashioned of fourteen-karat gold.

Lola kept Munich's leading dressmaker so busy that the woman soon had no time for other clients. The fabrics for the gowns and other clothing made for the King's greedy young mistress were imported from France; Lola did not bother to look at the bills but turned them over to Ludwig for payment.

The most significant change in Lola was in her temperament. She became arrogant, imperious, and quarrelsome. She demanded perfection from her servants and treated them with blistering scorn when they failed to live up to her expectations. The shopkeepers of Munich soon learned to dread her, and in spite of the business she brought them were not eager to be of assistance.

"King Ludwig thinks so highly of her," wrote a French actor who had known Lola in Paris and who stopped off for a visit with her in Munich, "that she behaves as though she had royal blood flowing through her own veins." The observation was shrewd.

It was not long before Lola's conduct incensed the whole city. One morning, out for a canter alone, she saw an elderly man on the path ahead of her riding at a slower pace. When he failed to move out of her way fast enough to suit her, Lola drew abreast, crowded him, and slashed at him with her riding crop until he faltered.

As it turned out, her outraged victim was a prominent member of the nobility, a Baron von Emmenthaler, who was so angry that he protested in person to the King, demanding that the perpetrator of the crime against him be punished. Ludwig managed to placate his distinguished subject, and the censor prevented news of the incident from leaking to the press. But the Emmenthaler family did not remain silent, and the story spread to other European capitals.

It was followed a month or so later by an even uglier incident. Ludwig had given Lola a large dog, and every evening after the King left her villa, Lola took the animal for a stroll. It was customary then, as now, for the owner of a pet to keep the animal leashed when walking on city streets. Lola chose to disregard the practice and enjoyed allowing her dog to roam at will.

One evening a tradesman making a late delivery emerged into the Theresienstrasse just as Lola and her dog were passing. The animal, for reasons of its own, took offense and lunged at the stranger. The tradesman tried to protect himself and struck at the dog, infuriating Lola. Wielding the dog's leather leash like a whip, she beat the man with it, opening several cuts on his face.

The incident was witnessed by a number of pedestrians, and

the story of the whipping spread swiftly. The tradesman was urged to seek retribution in court, but he apparently felt he could not obtain justice if he filed suit against the King's favorite. His working class friends decided to take matters into their own hands, and one afternoon a threatening mob gathered outside Lola's villa.

It happened that Ludwig was visiting her at the time; a company of infantry was summoned from the nearby barracks, and the crowd was dispersed. Ludwig subsequently called the tradesman to the palace and gave him a purse to quiet him, but the damage had been done. The common people of Munich were now firm in their antipathy toward the young foreign woman who considered herself above the law.

Lola's increasing boredom is a factor that may have helped inspire her entry into the political arena. She had no real friends in Munich other than Ludwig, and her mode of life made it difficult for her to expand her circle. There is no indication, to be sure, that she intended to use her intervention in politics as a stepping-stone to a more active social life. Her involvement did, however, occupy her time and satisfy a newly acquired taste for power.

She began by persuading King Ludwig to grant his subjects greater freedom of assemblage. A new royal decree to that effect was issued. A few days later a meeting was held in a Munich working-class district, and speaker after speaker urged members of the audience not to pay rent for their apartments—squalid slum dwellings unfit for habitation. Since the apartment houses belonged to the archdiocese, Auxiliary Bishop von Moellner of Munich promptly went to the palace and protested vigorously.

Next came a relaxation of press censorship, which proved as harmful to Lola as to those she wanted to supplant. The press immediately became critical of Prime Minister von Abel and of the Church, urging that the Jesuits be removed from the all-powerful board of censors. Three of the city's newspapers also launched attacks on Lola, and indirectly on the King, pointing out that Lola was living in great luxury while loyal Bavarians were unable to find work and were suffering hardships.

Lola persisted in her campaign, however, and soon was meddling in every aspect of Bavarian domestic life. Officials of Church and State were annoyed, but regarded her as nothing more than a temporary nuisance; no one in a position of authority seemed to consider her a threat to the Establishment. That situation changed when authorities found out that Lola was developing an enthusiastic following in the student body at the university, where reform-minded younger Jesuits were believed to be inciting the students, although the secret police could unearth no positive evidence.

Prime Minister von Abel discussed the matter with the King several times, but Ludwig would neither agree to curb Lola's influence nor permit his chief of government to criticize her. The most popular story of the period appeared in London, Paris, and Berlin newspapers. According to this account, Abel lost his temper when his pleas were rejected, and said to the Elector, "Then the Montez woman is King!"

"Yes," Ludwig supposedly replied, putting an end to the conversation, "she *is* King!"

By early 1847 the authorities, well aware of the danger that Lola posed, launched their counterattacks. The senior Jesuits investigated her past; the reports they received, however inaccurate, were damaging. In January, 1847, thousands of copies of an anonymous pamphlet about Lola flooded the cities of Bavaria. Ludwig ordered the document suppressed, but the secret police were unable to prevent its dissemination.

Lola, the pamphlet said, had been born the daughter of a French mother and an English father. She had earned her living as a streetwalker in Paris, but was driven from France when a prominent journalist died in a duel fought for her favors. She then fled to England, where she became a paid spy for the Freemasons, who had sent her to Bavaria in order to disrupt the government and economy of that devoutly Catholic country.

There were many gaps in the pamphlet's logic, but large numbers of Ludwig's citizens believed what they read, and for the first time Lola was subjected to active discrimination. Bakers, greengrocers, and butchers refused to sell to her servants until Ludwig personally sent an aide-de-camp to the shopkeepers and threatened reprisals. Insults were painted late every night on the walls of her villa; a squad of troops of the royal household guards was posted outside the house.

There were some situations in which Ludwig was powerless to intervene on Lola's behalf. Sermons condemning his mistress were delivered in churches all over Bavaria, including Munich's cathedral. The archbishop replied to Ludwig's protest with a brief statement to the effect that "the people must be protected from scarlet women." Conservative university students banded together in opposition to Lola, and the younger Jesuits, alarmed by the ugly feelings that were being aroused, warned the King that there might be riots and bloodshed on the campus.

But Lola could do no wrong in the eyes of Ludwig, who continued to give her his unhesitating support. According to one widespread story, Abel and representatives of the Church asked Queen Theresa to use whatever influence she possessed. She went to her husband, who refused to listen to her, and then to Lola, who treated her with great courtesy but would not withdraw from public life. If this meeting between the Queen and Lola Montez ever took place, there is no record of the event.

The anti-Montez campaign intensified, and so many copies of cartoons ridiculing Lola flooded Bavaria that an enterprising Berlin publisher brought out a book containing fifty of them.

Matters came to a head late in January, 1847, when King Ludwig issued a new royal decree that removed two government departments, those of Education and Public Worship, from the jurisdiction of Prime Minister von Abel. They were placed in the charge of one Baron von Schrenk, an apostate who had recently returned from living abroad. In effect Ludwig's decree removed control of the schools from the hands of the Jesuits and publicly humiliated the Prime Minister. Neither Abel nor the senior members of the Society of Jesus could tolerate such a defeat, and the

Prime Minister entered into an extraordinary correspondence with the monarch.

Ludwig not only refuted all of Abel's arguments, he revealed his intention to make Lola a member of the Bavarian nobility. As a preliminary step in that direction, he signed and published letters patent that granted her the status and rights of Bavarian citizenship.

Abel played his final card. In order for the letter patent to become legal, the countersignature of a cabinet member was required. The Prime Minister summoned his ministers to a secret council of war. A letter written at this meeting was sent to the King, and copies were thoughtfully provided for the edification of the foreign press. This remarkable document read:

Sir:

There are circumstances in which men invested with the inappreciable confidence of their sovereign, and charged with the direction of affairs, are called upon to renounce their most sacred duties or to expose themselves, at the bidding of their conscience, to the risk of incurring the displeasure of their beloved monarch. This is the sad necessity to which your ministers find themselves reduced by the royal determination to grant to Señora Lola Montez letters of naturalization. We are incapable of forgetting the oaths we took to Your Majesty, and our resolution has never been for a moment doubtful. The proposed naturalization of Señora Montez was openly characterized by Councillor von Maurer as the greatest calamity with which Bavaria could be afflicted. This was the conviction of the entire Council and the opinion of all Your Majesty's faithful subjects.

Since December last the eyes of the nation have been fixed on Munich. The respect for the sovereign becomes weaker and weaker in all minds, because on all sides nothing is heard but the most bitter blame and disapprobation. National feeling is wounded: Bavaria believes itself to be governed by a foreign woman, whose reputation is branded in public opinion. Men like the Bishop of Augsburg, whose devotion to Your Majesty cannot be disputed, daily shed bitter tears for what is passing before their eyes; the ministers of Interior and of Finance have witnessed his profound affliction. The Prince Bishop of Breslau, hearing a rumor that he has countenanced the actual state of affairs, has written to persons in Munich formally and most emphatically expressing his disapprobation. His letter is no longer a secret, and soon will be known to the whole country.

Foreign journals every day relate the most scandalous anecdotes, and make the most degrading attacks on Your Majesty. The copy of the *Ulner Chronik*, which we here subjoin, is a proof of our assertions.

In vain do the police attempt to halt the circulation of these journals, which are everywhere read with avidity. The impression which they leave on men's minds is by no means doubtful. It is the same from Berchtesgaden and Passau to Aschaffenburg and Zweibrücken. It is the same throughout Europe, in the cabin of the poor and the manor house of the rich. It is not alone the glory and well-being of Your Majesty's government that is compromised, but the very existence of royalty itself. It is this which explains the joy of the enemies of the throne, and the profound grief and despair of all who are faithfully attached to Your Majesty, and who are alive to the dangers greater than any to which it has been exposed.

In this state of affairs, it is inevitable that what is taking place here will influence the army, and if this bulwark should give way, where would be our resource?

The statement which the undersigned, whose hearts are torn with anguish, venture to place before Your Majesty, is not the product of terrified imaginations, but of observations which each has made within the circle of his attributions during several months. The effect of these circumstances in the ensuing parliamentary session may easily be foreseen.

Each of the undersigned is ready to sacrifice for Your Majesty his fortune and his life. Your ministers believe that they have given you proofs of their fidelity and attachment, but it is for them a doubly sacred duty to point out to Your Majesty the ever-increasing danger of this situation. We beg you to listen to our humble prayer and not to suppose that it is dictated by any desire to thwart your royal will. It is directed only against a state of affairs which threatens to destroy the fair fame, power, and future happiness of a beloved King.

Your ministers are convinced, after earnest deliberation, that if Your Majesty should not deign to give ear to their supplications, they are compelled to resign the positions to which the kindness and confidence of their sovereign has called them, and to pray

Your Majesty to remove the portfolios with which they are entrusted.

Signed
von Abel, First Minister
von Gumpenberg
von Seinsheim
von Dordelshelm, S. J.
von Giese
von Bulow

King Ludwig still hoped to avoid a showdown. When he received the communication, he asked Abel if there were any other copies. He was assured that none existed. The following day the *Augsburger Zeitung* printed the complete text, and it was explained to the outraged monarch that the press had inadvertently gained possession of the original draft, which von Giese had failed to lock in his desk. Within the next forty-eight hours, newspapers in London, Paris, and Berlin reprinted the letter in its entirety, and the battle Ludwig had wanted to avoid was joined.

[CHAPTER XIII]

At the direction of King Ludwig an aide-de-camp, Count Adrian von Ressler, took the ministers' letter to Lola Montez at her villa. Still following instructions, he awaited her reply. Ressler, who later accompanied his monarch into exile, described her reaction in a letter to his wife. Lola, he said, turned pale as she began to read, but in a few moments her normal coloring returned, and she smiled. Soon she was giggling, then laughing so heartily that the tears rolling down her cheeks caused the kohl she had painted on her eyelids and lashes to run.

"Tell His Majesty," Ressler quotes her as saying, "that I cannot write in earnest about something this absurd. Tell him Abel and the others are even bigger fools than I thought."

Ludwig could not regard the affair as a laughing matter. Had the contents of the letter been kept secret, it might have been possible to work out some sort of compromise. But the publicity everywhere in Europe had been so great that the Elector felt his dignity as a monarch to be at stake. He acted accordingly. Writing a curt note to his cabinet, he demanded that the threat be withdrawn forthwith, lest he be forced to dismiss all his ministers.

Abel and his subordinates had climbed onto a slender limb, too, and now found themselves unable to return to the solid trunk of the tree. Rejecting the King's demand, they appeared together at the palace to submit their resignations. Ludwig proceeded to compound the foolishness by refusing to accept their letters, and instead handed each minister a royal notice of dismissal.

The Church took no active part in the matter, even though one of the ministers, Dordelshelm, was a Jesuit priest. The bishops of Bavaria and the senior Jesuits, not wanting to make a martyr of Lola Montez, had decided to lie low: if unopposed, the King would behave as he had in the past and soon grow tired of her. A prominent professor at the university, Gerhard von Lassaulx, two of whose sons were junior Jesuits, knew nothing of this strategy and delivered a furious assault on the King during the course of a lecture being delivered to more than 300 undergraduates.

The more conservative of the students marched from the lecture hall to Lola's villa, arriving in such numbers that the small squad of soldiers stationed outside did not even try to disperse them. Lola appeared on a balcony to observe the demonstration, and in a light-hearted gesture raised the glass of champagne she was holding in a salute to the students.

The catcalls of the students grew louder and more insulting. Suddenly there was dead silence: Ludwig I had appeared on the balcony behind Lola, convinced that his presence would break up the demonstration. Instead the crowd grew noisier and larger. Within an hour, according to an official police estimate, more than 10,000 people were crammed into the Theresienstrasse.

Count von Rechberg, who had accompanied the King to Lola's villa, reported that the people were in an ugly mood, and the commander of the guard detail urged Ludwig not to return to the palace without adequate protection. A courier was sent to the barracks, and within minutes two full troops of royal household hussars rode onto the scene with drawn sabers. They provided Ludwig with an escort, enabling him to return to the palace without further difficulty.

He had been challenged, all the same, and everyone in Europe seemed to know it. According to the London *Herald*, that night was the first time in Bavarian history it had been necessary to protect an Elector from his own subjects. The *Times* published an editorial castigating the people of Munich for the lack of respect they had shown the King; the staunch royalist organ of Prussia, the *Berliner Abendpost,* said the same thing in stronger language. In Paris, Girardin's *La Presse* said the incident marked the beginning of the end for Ludwig, and indeed March 1, 1847, has generally been regarded as the day Ludwig started to lose control of his subjects.

One interesting sidelight of the affair was the friendship that developed between Lola and Professor von Lassaulx. Lola wrote him a letter, asking him to call on her so that she could explain her side of the situation, and Lassaulx' curiosity inspired him to accept the invitation. Lola undoubtedly exerted her celebrated charm to the utmost, and Lassaulx apparently succumbed to it. He had too much integrity to switch sides and continued to support the dismissed ministers, but after several meetings with Lola he claimed he "understood" her position and even became active on her behalf, arguing with fellow faculty members and other intellectuals that she was an innocent pawn shrewdly manipulated by Ludwig.

Lola soon discovered that she had good friends in the student body, too. Two undergraduate liberal leaders, Fritz Peissner and Count Adolf Hirschenberg, came to her with an offer to form a new fraternal corps devoted to her protection. If Lola had been wise, she would have discouraged any further polarization of public opinion; instead, she was so flattered that she not only accepted the offer but gave the students a substantial sum of money to purchase distinctive headbands and sashes for their corps. Unfortunately there was enough money left over to enable Peissner to purchase quantities of firearms for Lola's defense.

Meanwhile Ludwig had the task of forming a new cabinet, and to show he meant business, he kept the folio of Prime Minister himself. His choice for the Ministry of the Interior, Baron zu Rhein, was a wise one; the Baron was known as a devoted supporter of the Church, and his appointment would placate the conservatives. As the senior Jesuits well knew, however, the naming of the Baron was a meaningless gesture. Zu Rhein was elderly and verged on senility; he would do whatever Ludwig—and Lola—requested. Luigi Zenetti, a wealthy commoner of Italian descent who was an outspoken liberal, was made Minister of Finance, and the army was pacified by the appointment of its most popular hero, Major General Maximilian von Hohenhausen, as Minister of War.

The most significant appointment was that of Baron Heinrich von Maurer as Minister of Justice. The Baron not only corresponded with Victor Hugo and other French moderates, but had written a number of essays for French and English journals of liberal persuasion. Worst of all in the eyes of the conservatives, he was a Protestant, the first non-Catholic ever to be given a portfolio as a minister in the government of Bavaria. Maurer, too, had an opportunity to calm ruffled waters, but like Lola he took a firm and defiant stand. In his first public statement he declared that the rule of the Jesuits had come to an end, a sentiment that the conservatives in general, and members of the senior Jesuit hierarchy in particular, failed to appreciate.

Maurer also countersigned Lola's naturalization decree, making her a Bavarian citizen and clearing the way for the honors the King wanted to bestow on her. Ludwig acted with almost indecent haste, publishing the new patent that raised her to the peerage on March 4, 1847, only three days after the new Minister of Justice had countersigned the decree.

Lola was made Countess of Landsberg and Baroness Rosenthal, "Countess" being the senior title. She was listed in the registry of Bavarian nobility as Maria Dolores Porris y Montez, the daughter of an officer in the Spanish army and a lady from Cuba. Ludwig also made her a canoness of the order of St. Theresa, the most aristocratic ladies' organization in Bavaria, and neither he nor Lola seemed in the least embarrassed by the fact that Queen Theresa was the head of the order. The King gave his mistress an annuity of 20,000 gold florins per year, the equivalent of more than $200,000 per year today. Overnight she became independently wealthy. Still not satisfied, he ordered a new palace built for his favorite in the Barenstrasse, and commissioned the painting of her portrait, which he gave a place of honor in his own palace gallery.

The new Countess of Landsberg had acquired instant social standing, at least in Ludwig's eyes and her own, and her social life changed accordingly. She held a nightly reception at her villa, and members of the aristocracy, Bavarian businessmen who wanted favors or assistance of some sort from the Crown, and the senior officers of foreign legations simultancously came to the same conclusion: it would be wise to put in regular appearances there.

Ludwig himself showed up faithfully every night, for at least an hour or two, and when his new ministers began to appear as well, Bavarians and foreigners realized that the villa on the Theresienstrasse had become the nation's power center. Royal and ministerial decisions were made there, and an American importer said in a letter to the New York *Post,*

It is impossible to engage in any endeavor in Munich, including the most routine commercial transaction, unless one first obtains the sanction of King Ludwig's favorite. Anyone who fails to go to her house, kiss her hand and sample the lavish food and drink she serves, had best go to some other country. Only those at whom this former dancer smiles are recognized and approved. The lady can do no wrong.

The opposition, which included former Prime Minister von Abel and the members of his cabinet, made the mistake of redoubling their attacks on Lola instead of waiting for the Elector to recover from his infatuation. By giving Ludwig no choice, they drove him still closer to Lola, who now had his undeviating support at all times and in all matters.

Lola had become the single most powerful force in Bavaria, but there were signs that serious trouble was brewing for her. The student corps sworn to defend her, which called itself the Alemannia, became involved in brawls with the rest of the student body, in spite of strenuous efforts made by the younger Jesuits to preserve the peace. These riots became increasingly violent, and when university authorities appealed to the government for help, Ludwig stationed a regiment of infantry in battle dress on the campus. The riots stopped, but the atmosphere was that of an occupied enclave in time of war.

The outside world was astonished, amused, or disgusted by the spectacle; certainly Lola Montez became the most notorious woman living. Had she ignored the gossip, she might have risen above the storm, but she was temperamentally incapable of closing her eyes and ears—and above all, her mouth—when under siege. She made the mistake of writing a letter to the *Times* of London in which she lashed out furiously at the Jesuits. The order, she said, had made Bavaria the headquarters for its worldwide operations: the Society of Jesus was engaged in a monstrous plot to capture the governmental apparatus of virtually every civilized country on earth. Only her own firm stand, she declared, had aborted the scheme; the world owed her a debt of gratitude.

Intelligent people everywhere knew that her story was absurd, but the ignorant seized on the tale to verify their own prejudices. Men who held posts of authority in many countries were forced to agree with Prime Minister von Metternich of Austria, who wrote that this woman was endowed with a far greater capacity for creating great mischief on an international scale than most people realized.

Lola not only relished the furor she created, she went out of her way to fan the flames of controversy. One evening in April, 1847, patrons of the Court Theatre saw her seated in the royal box, gorgeously gowned, her jewels including a tiara ablaze with gems. Then two aides were seen at the rear of the box, and a moment later King Ludwig appeared. As he moved forward to take his place beside his mistress, everyone in the theater—with one exception—paid him the respect due his position by rising. Lola remained seated, thereby serving notice that she was not subject to the unwritten laws governing the conduct of other people. This seemingly trivial gesture was one of her worst tactical errors, and even those of Ludwig's subjects who had tried to avoid taking sides now began to cast their lot against her.

Her lack of respect for the Elector inadvertently harmed the cause of hard-pressed royalists in many other nations. The forces of republicanism were growing, and socialist newspapers in France, England, the Netherlands, and elsewhere hailed Lola's defiance of protocol. Louis Philippe, the French king who would be deposed in the revolution of 1848, wanted his censors to prohibit the mentioning of Lola's name in print. Much to his subsequent regret, he was dissuaded.

At the end of May, 1847, Ludwig followed his annual custom of leaving Munich for the summer and went by train to his summer palace at Bruckenau, accompanied by more than fifty members of his court. He was sufficiently aware of the rising tide of public feeling to take precautions: three companies of armed troops were on board the train to make certain that the King's majesty would not be disturbed.

Following the King on a private train of her own was Lola, supposedly traveling incognito. It would not have been difficult to guess the identity of the woman dressed in form-fitting black, a heavy veil over her face, accompanied by a retinue of servants and escorted by a detail of secret police in civilian clothes. The news of her journey traveled faster than her train. At a number of stations along the route, crowds gathered, and when the engineer slowed his speed, men and women screamed insults at her. Lola remained hidden behind closed curtains.

A far more serious incident occurred in the town of Bamberg, where her presence virtually guaranteed the outbreak of violence. A strong contingent of young Catholic men was on hand when she arrived, and the waiting mayor escorted her to her carriage to the accompaniment of a loud chorus of hisses and boos. As the carriage started to pull away from the station, someone threw a rock, which was followed by a deluge of stones. In a moment the open coach was surrounded by a mob, and the mayor could not make himself heard above the uproar.

Lola, never one to accept a threatening situation easily, took matters into her own hands. She opened the leather traveling case she was carrying and calmly removed two large pistols, which she cocked. The crowd grew quiet as she climbed onto the seat. Then, according to the press reports printed around the world, she promised to shoot the next man who threw a rock at her, and dared the crowd to attack again. There was nothing she would enjoy more, she said, than proving her marksmanship.

No one accepted her challenge. She sat down, still clutching the pistols, and the carriage started to move again. Meanwhile word of her plight had spread swiftly, and a large band of young Protestants started to march to her rescue. Bloodshed appeared inevitable, and Lola was fortunate to reach her hotel before the rioting began. Within minutes after she went to her suite, the two groups clashed in the street below.

Only the intervention of the mayor prevented Lola from making matters still worse by appearing on her balcony to watch the riot. A strong contingent of troops soon appeared, and the rioters were routed. No accurate list of casualties was ever published, and no news of the affair appeared in any Bavarian newspaper. London accounts, which were copied by the American press, said that "dozens" had been hurt, while the more sensational Paris newspapers claimed "hundreds" of injuries.

The Bamberg incident further inflamed Bavarian public opinion, and pamphlets denouncing Lola appeared with such regularity that it soon became obvious that the secret police were working in league with the opposition. Karl von Abel later denied that he himself had been the author of several of the pamphlets. Only through the connivance of the police, however, was it possible for a scurrilous book about Lola to be circulated in Bavaria. The volume had been written by one of her former servants, a man named Papon, and published in France, where it had enjoyed a brief popularity. The translation into German now produced an even more spectacular book, not only telling the story of Lola's numerous imaginary affairs, but accusing her of having been mistress of the revels at depraved orgies.

If the subject of the book knew of its popularity in Bavaria, she gave no sign. She and Ludwig were inseparable, and every evening she danced for him—often in the presence of courtiers and diplomats who were forced to applaud her performance.

In August, when Ludwig went on to another of his summer

residences, Lola returned to Munich. It had not been possible to build her the new home Ludwig had commissioned in time for early occupation, so a small palace on the Barenstrasse which had belonged to one of Ludwig's uncles prior to his death was turned over to her. Vast sums had been spent on the redecoration of the palace, which had been good enough for Bavarian royalty but was inadequate according to the new, high standards of the Countess of Landsberg.

Lola's bathroom in the palace was the talk of the Continent. Rose-colored glass had been installed in the windows so that the room glowed with a soft light. The sunken tub, made of marble, was a priceless work of art that had been excavated and repolished in Rome. All of the fixtures were gold, and a special dressing table mirror, seven feet high and five and one half feet wide, had been made to Lola's specifications in Venice and transported at great expense. On the bathroom floor were rugs of fur. A special water softener had been imported from England for Lola's baths.

Still undeterred by the commotion she was causing, Lola went out of her way to infuriate the populace. Her student admirers gave a dinner in her honor, and only with difficulty could the secret police persuade them to hold the affair in a beer garden on the outskirts of the city rather than at a restaurant in the heart of Munich, where a riot would have broken out. Lola would have been wise to call off the dinner, but instead she rode to it in an open carriage, wearing a feminine version of her followers' student uniform. University graduates assumed she was mocking a tradition that dated back to the Middle Ages, and any support she had enjoyed in their ranks melted away.

The banquet's repercussions were worse than any riot could have caused. The opposition was constantly searching for new ways to discredit Lola, and a few days after the dinner a new pamphlet appeared, purporting to tell what had happened at the party: everyone had drunk too much, and then Lola had rewarded her followers by going off with them, one by one, into a sumptuously furnished bedchamber set up for the occasion in a building adjacent to the beer garden. Thousands of respectable people were duly horrified by the story, and even the most loyal of the King's supporters began to wonder if his foreign friend wasn't threatening Ludwig's comfort and safety.

By the time the King returned to Munich in September, the country was in an uproar. Ludwig's supporters held a meeting in the Bavarian highlands to discuss ways and means of getting rid of the Countess of Landsberg. More than 150 distinguished gentlemen were present, as were several secret police spies, who gave the King a full list of those in attendance. Ludwig promptly demoted those who held places in the government and retired several high-ranking army officers. All of these men transferred their allegiance to the opposition.

Since it was dangerous to oppose Lola Montez openly, a new approach was devised to circumvent the royal wrath. A rally was held in Bamberg, at which speaker after speaker extolled the virtues of Queen Theresa. Nothing derogatory was said about Lola; in fact, no mention was made of her name. The King could hardly punish people for praising his wife, who continued to live under his roof in Munich, so no arrests were made. The success of the Bamberg experiment inspired similar rallies in virtually every other city and town in the country.

Queen Theresa was embarrassed by these expressions of loyalty. Apparently still hoping that Ludwig would lose interest in the foreign dancer, she wanted to do nothing that might inspire him to give Lola still more support. But Theresa was a pawn in the hands of the opposition. Although she wrote privately to Abel and several others, urging an end to such demonstrations, the demonstrations continued.

It was at this point that Prime Minister von Metternich of Austria, who received regular reports from his own agents across the Bavarian border, predicted that Ludwig would lose his throne, if not his life; and that Lola Montez would be stoned to death by a Bavarian mob.

[CHAPTER XIV]

In 1847 and 1848 the newspapers of Europe and America accepted as a fact that Lola Montez was a liberal of deep convictions and that her influence was transforming Bavaria from an ultraconservative monarchy into a progressive nation that embodied the best of the democratic process in its government.

Seen from the perspective of more than a century and a quarter, the idea of Lola as a liberal crusader seems unlikely in the extreme: never in her life before or after the Bavarian episode did she show more than a passing interest in politics or devotion to the cause of individual liberties.

This is not to deny that her endless, uninformed meddling in Bavarian affairs had its effect. Ministers of state were dismissed at her behest, and nonentities were raised to positions of trust because she smiled. Her battle with the conservative statesmen and politicians of the country, not to mention the senior members of the Jesuit hierarchy, was fought in earnest.

Bavaria moved in a more liberal direction, certainly, during the months that Lola was the power behind the throne. Circumstances and her own extraordinary character had given Lola the opportunity to star in a new role. Lola, being Lola, played it to the hilt. Unexpectedly she found herself in a position of power because King Ludwig came to her for advice. Perhaps she was weary of being a *femme fatale*, at least for the moment. In any event, she relished the new drama. Always an extremist, she performed in it with a fervor that not only caught the world's attention but convinced much of it that she was the potent advocate of freedom she seemed to be, rather than a meddler playing with dangerous fires she did not understand.

Lola went through all of the political motions, to be sure. Bavarian politicians and diplomats from other nations filled her salon. She gave directions, heedless of their consequences. She conferred daily with Ludwig, freely dispensing the advice the foolish, bemused man sought from her. Never before had she acted on such an enormous stage before so large an audience.

It may be significant that no memoranda or other documents written by Lola have survived her "reign." Her advice, like that of the mistresses of Louis XIV in France, appears to have been given verbally, as were her instructions to the ministers of state whom she treated like house servants. Lola wrote no position papers, made no public addresses, and attended no cabinet meetings. And in all probability her theater of operations in Bavaria was unique.

The extent to which Lola Montez was responsible for the policies of the Bavarian government that in 1847 and early 1848 made it the most liberal in Europe is debatable. The question was complicated in Lola's own day by the attitude of liberals in many countries who regarded her as a heroine. As for Lola herself, unsuccessful as a dancer, she was all the more eager to accept credit for political reforms.

Writers for scores of republican and liberal newspapers and periodicals made a pilgrimage to Munich during the year and a half that Lola was the uncrowned ruler of Bavaria. She granted audiences to all of them. Interviewed several times each week, she saw her name placed constantly before the public. She also took bows for every government act that granted greater freedom to the individual or eased the plight of the working man.

Again, it was only during this brief period of Lola's life that she showed any deep or sustained concern for the welfare of anyone other than herself. Her admirers have suggested that Dujarier taught her to admire and respect the common man and that through his influence she developed the desire to help the struggling masses. Bavarians—even Ludwig's supporters—recognized no such desires.

Lola's ultimate downfall may be attributed, at least in part, to her failure to win allies. The new members of Ludwig's cabinet should have been her strongest supporters, but she antagonized them by insisting to the world's press that she alone was responsible for every reform. Maurer and Rhein were proud of their accomplishments, and it galled them to see Lola standing in the spotlight while they looked on.

Maurer particularly resented Lola's informing her interviewers that she had originated the legislation granting greater liberty to Protestants, permitting freedom of assemblage, and halting the power encroachment of the Jesuits. Only a few of his fellow Bavarians knew of these substantial contributions of Maurer's to the cause of freedom, and beyond the borders of Bavaria he was still virtually unknown. "The Spaniard is so greedy," he told his brother-in-law in a letter written in late September of 1847, "that she steals the glory belonging to everyone. She thinks of my colleagues and me as creatures in a class with her household majordomo, and I do not know how much longer we can tolerate this condition. Our problem is made so much worse because the King will hear no complaints against her, and on occasion I wonder if he, too, thinks of her as the savior of the country."

In the autumn of 1847, after the new law granting greater freedom of expression to the press had been pushed through the Parliament and signed by Ludwig, Lola discovered that the sword of liberalism cut two ways. The opposition press, now free to say what they pleased about her, attacked her with unconcealed venom. She was so angered by this assault that she tried to persuade the King to crack down on the newspapers, but this time he did not act on her behalf. Even the infatuated Ludwig knew he could not revoke these rights just granted without making himself look foolish. So few people knew of Lola's attempt to restore full censorship, however, that her reputation remained untarnished in liberal circles.

Ludwig's ministers soon found they could not function in an atmosphere Lola tried to control, and in December, 1847, the quarrel came to a showdown. Ludwig continued to offer his mistress unqualified support; Maurer and Rhein resigned, forcing a cabinet reshuffle. Prince Wallerstein, the Elector's elderly cousin, was recalled from his post as ambassador to Paris and became the head of the Foreign Ministry. The key post—Minister of the Interior, who controlled the secret police—went to Count Emil von Berks.

This appointment convinced anyone who still needed convincing that Lola was a dissolute woman. Berks, who changed mistresses as frequently as he changed his ruffled shirts, was a hard-drinking bachelor who had publicly disavowed Catholicism. He had been one of Lola's most ardent admirers since the early days of her sojourn in Munich, and the rumor that he was her secret lover was accepted at face value by many at the court who believed the King to be impotent. It has never been established to posterity's satisfaction that Lola and Berks actually had an affair, but there is ample evidence that they were good friends and that Lola's influence won Berks his powerful place in the cabinet. Berks, in turn, illegally silenced some of Lola's more vociferous critics, thereby broadening the rapidly increasing circle of her enemies.

So much that is contradictory was written about Lola during this climactic phase of her life that it is hard to gain an objective view of her. Most of her contemporaries loved or hated her, a few felt contempt for her, many envied her, and a handful quietly laughed at her. All wrote accordingly, impartial journalism being a rarity in mid-nineteenth century Europe. Thus the portrait of Lola that emerges from these claims and counterclaims is often out of focus.

Fortunately George Henry Francis, a distinguished English journalist who later became editor-in-chief of the London *Post*, was in Munich during six months of Lola's visit. An article of his published in *Fraser's* Magazine in January, 1848, may well be the clearest and least biased of contemporary accounts. It read in part:

The house of Lola Montez at Munich presents an elegant contrast to the large, cold, lumbering mansions which are the greatest defect in the general architecture of the city. It is a *bijou*, rebuilt for her under her own eye by her own architect, Herr Metzger, at Number 19 Barenstrasse, and is unique in its simplicity and lightness. It is of two stories, and allowing for its plainness, is in the Italian style. Elegant bronze balconies from the upper windows, designed by herself, relieve the plainness of the exterior; and long, muslin curtains, slightly tinted, and drawn close so as to cover the windows, add a transparent, shell-like lightness to the effect. Any English gentleman (Señorita Montez has a great respect for England and the English) can, on presenting his card, tour the interior; but the house is not a "show place." The interior surpasses everything in Munich, where decorative painting and internal fitting has been carried almost to perfection.

We are not going to write an upholsterer's catalogue, but as everything was done by the immediate choice and under the personal direction of the fair Lola, the general characteristics of the place will serve to illustrate her character. Such a tigress, one would think, would scarcely choose so beautiful a den. The smallness of the palace precludes much splendor. Its place is supplied by French elegance, Munich art, and English comfort. The walls of the chief room are exquisitely painted by the first artists from designs found in Herculaneum and Pompeii, but selected with great taste by Lola Montez. The furniture is not gaudily rich, but elegant enough to harmonize with the decorations. A small winter room, adjoining the larger one, is fitted up, quite in the English style, with papered walls, sofas, easy chairs, all of elegant shape. A chimney, with a first-rate grate of English manufacture, and rich, thick carpets and rugs, complete the illusion.

The walls are hung with pictures, among them a Raphael, a Titian and a Rubens. There are also some of the best works of modern German painters; a good portrait of the King; and a very bad one of the mistress of the mansion.

The rest of the establishment bespeaks equally the exquisite taste of the fair owner. The drawing rooms and her boudoir are perfect gems. Books, not of a frivolous kind, borrowed from the royal library, lie about, and help to show the habits of this modern Amazon. Her reading habits lie in the direction of biography, history, and economics; she eschews fiction. Add to her belongings a piano and a guitar, on both of which she accompanies herself with considerable taste and some skill, and an embroidery frame, at which she produces works that put to shame the best of those exhibited for sale in England.

So you see she is positively compelled at times to resort to some amusement becoming of her sex, as a relief from those more masculine or unworthy occupations in which, according to her enemies, she emulates alternately the example of Peter the Great and Catherine II.

The rest of the appointments of the place are in keeping: the coach-house and stabling (her equipages are extremely modest and her household no more numerous or ostentatious than those of any gentlewoman of great means), the culinary offices, and an exquisite bathroom, into which the light comes tinted with rose color. At the back of the little palace is a large flower garden, in which, during the summer, most of the political consultations between the fair Countess and her sovereign are held.

As for her habits of life, they are simple. She eats little, and of plain food, cooked in the English fashion; drinks little, keeps good hours, rises early, and labors much. The morning, before and after breakfast, is devoted to what we must call semi-public business. The innumerable letters she receives and affairs she has to arrange, keep herself and her secretary constantly employed for several hours. At breakfast she holds a sort of *levée* of persons of all sorts—ministers past and present, professors, artists, English strangers, and foreigners from all parts of the world. As is usual with women of an active mind, she is a great talker; but although an egotist, and with her share of the vanity of a beautiful woman, she understands the art of conversation sufficiently never to be wearisome. Indeed, although capable of violent though evanescent passions—of deep but not revengeful animosities, and occasionally of trivialities and weaknesses very often found in persons suddenly raised to great power—she can be, and almost always is, a very charming person and a delightful companion. Her manners are distinguished, she is a graceful and hospitable hostess, and she understands the art of dressing to perfection.

The fair despot is passionately fond of homage. She is merciless in her man-killing propensities, and those gentlemen attending her *levées* or her *soirées*, who are perhaps too much absorbed in politics or art to be enamored of her personal charms, willingly pay respect to her mental attractions and conversational powers.

On the other hand, Lola Montez has many of the faults recorded of others in like situations. She loves power for its own sake. She is too hasty and too steadfast in her dislikes. She has not sufficiently learned to curb the passion which seems natural to her Spanish blood. She is capricious, and quite capable, when her temper is inflamed, of rudeness which, however, she is the first to regret and to apologize for.

She has one absorbing idea which poisons her peace. She is devoting her life to the extirpation of the Jesuits, root and branch, from Bavaria. She is too ready to believe in their active influence, and too easily overlooks their passive influence. Every one whom she does not like, her prejudice transforms into a Jesuit. She truly believes that Jesuits stare at her in the streets, and peep at her from the corners of her rooms. All the world, adverse to herself, are puppets moved to mock and annoy her by these dark and invisible agents. At the same time she has, doubtless, good cause for this animosity; but these restless suspicions are a weakness quite incompatible with the strength of mind, force of character, and determination of purpose she exhibits in other respects . . .

As a political character, she holds an important position in Bavaria, besides having agents and correspondents in various Courts of Europe. The King generally visits her in the morning, from eleven until twelve or one o'clock; sometimes she is summoned to the nearby palace to consult with him, or with the ministers on state affairs. It is probable that during her habits of intimacy with some of the principal political writers of Paris, she acquired that knowledge of politics and insight into the maneuvers of diplomatists and statesmen which she now turns to advantage in her new sphere of action.

On foreign politics she seems to have very clear ideas; and her novel and powerful method of expressing them has a great charm for the King, who has himself a comprehensive mind. On the internal politics of Bavaria she has the good sense not to rely upon her own judgment, but to consult those whose studies and occupations qualify them to afford information. For the rest, she is treated by the political men of the country as a substantive power; and, however much they may secretly rebel against her influence, they at least find it good policy to acknowledge it.

Whatever indiscretions she may commit, she always keeps state secrets, and therefore can be consulted with perfect safety in cases where her original habits of thought render her of invaluable service. Acting under advice, which entirely accords with the King's own general principles, His Majesty has pledged himself to a course of steady, gradual improvement, which is calculated to increase the political freedom and material prosperity of his kingdom, without risking that unity of power, which in the present state of European affairs, is essential to its protection and advancement.

One thing much in the praise of Lola Montez is that although she really wields so much power, she never uses it either for the promotion of unworthy causes or, as other favorites have done, for corrupt purposes. Her creation as Countess of Landsberg, which has alienated her from some of her most honest liberal supporters, who wished her still to continue in rank, as well as in purposes, one of the people, while it has exasperated against her the powerless—because impoverished—nobility, was the unsolicited act of the King, legally effected with the voluntary consent of the Crown Prince.

Without entrenching too far upon a delicate subject, it may be added that the Countess is not regarded with contempt or detestation by either the male or female members of the royal family. Her income, including a recent addition from the King, is seventy thousand gold florins, or a little more than twenty thousand pounds per annum. While upon this subject of her position, it might be added that it is reported, on good authority, that the Queen of Bavaria (to whom the King has always paid the most scrupulous attentions due to her as his wife) very recently made a voluntary communication to her husband, apparently with the knowledge of the princes and other members of the royal family, that should the King desire at any future time, that the Countess should—as a matter of right—be presented at Court, the Queen would offer no obstacle . . .

The relation subsisting between the King of Bavaria and the Countess of Landsberg is not of a coarse or vulgar nature, no matter how many vicious falsehoods to the contrary have found their way into the public prints and have, therefore, been accepted as a matter of course by those who are not aware of the true nature of this intimacy. The King has a highly poetical mind, and sees his favorite through his imagination, which is endowed with a qualty of purity often found in romantics and idealists. Knowing perfectly well what her antecedents have been, he takes her as she is, and finding her an agreeable and intellectual companion, and as an honest, plain-speaking councillor, he fuses the reality with the ideal in one deep sentiment of affectionate respect.

The English journalist proved to be an accurate prophet. Lola acquired so much influence over King Ludwig that Queen Theresa had to swallow her own pride. On February 3, 1848, the former dancer was formally received at court. According to the report of many eyewitnesses, she was dressed in a gown of white satin edged in black, and wore two decorations on a sash of green silk. She curtsied before the throne of the King, then made an equally deep curtsy before the Queen. The two women exchanged fleeting smiles, but did not speak, and the audience came to an end.

The Court presentation was symbolic of the heights Lola had scaled, it now being universally recognized that she had become the single most important person in Bavaria. This consciousness of her power caused her foes to band together, liberal former ministers joining hands with their conservative predecessors. The younger Jesuits, realizing that their own influence was slipping, made themselves subservient to the senior Jesuits whose will they had flouted. Catholics and Protestants alike were dismayed over the influence wielded by a woman who readily admitted having been intimate with a number of men before captivating King Ludwig.

And so, at the very moment that Lola Montez rode the crest of her wave of power, forces too great for her to control were drawing together for the sole purpose of destroying her.

[CHAPTER XV]

The first of the socialist revolutions that shook Europe in 1848 broke out in February of that year in Paris. Overnight the monarchy was abolished, and a republic took its place. The thirty-year-old Karl Marx, whose *Communist Manifesto* was published that same year, was convinced that a new era was at hand. Insurrections broke out in nation after nation, independent grand duchy after principality; nearly everywhere the people were seizing the reins of power.

One exception was Bavaria, where the political earthquake that shook that country to its foundations might more accurately be called a counter-revolution. Its initial object was to end the rule of a woman who, whatever her motives, was the most liberalizing force in the nation's history. It was her meddling in matters beyond her depth that terminated Lola's affair and drove Ludwig from his throne; the very forces that Lola set in motion gained so much momentum they could not be halted.

It is significant to note that no serious effort was made to destroy the institution of the monarchy. There were few socialists or other radicals in Bavaria, and only a handful of extremists wanted to establish a republic. The reasons were not hard to find. Bavaria was a prosperous country, and even the poor were relatively well off. The peasants still formed the nation's backbone, the rich soil produced bumper crops, and no one went hungry, in part because prices were lower than in almost any other European country. There were no industrial slums, as yet, in Munich or any other Bavarian city, and although the workers were discontented, they were not yet sufficiently disturbed by their living conditions to engage in open revolt.

The people did, however, want improvements. Lola's domination of the King was so complete and she treated her growing band of enemies with such contempt that she became the natural target for dissidents. She had antagonized the Catholic majority, and most members of the Protestant minority were made uneasy by her moral standards. Politicians of every stripe hated her, and she had made no attempt to create any base for her power. Aside from the small group of students in the Alemannia, she had no popular support. Her strength rested exclusively on the authority she derived from the King; once Ludwig was maneuvered into a corner, Lola was isolated.

The crisis began on February 8, 1848, with the funeral of a man named Görres. A one-time revolutionary, he had become a mystic and had a large following among the conservatives who made up the political party that called itself the Ultramontane. Secret-police reports indicated that younger right-wing groups were spoiling for a fight, and a decree was issued forbidding the making of speeches at the funeral.

All four of the leading student corps—the Franconia, Bavaria, Isar, and Swabia—turned out in force for the event, however, and the young men marched through the streets of Munich together. They were joined by several thousand others, including working men, peasants, and middle-class youth. The fears of the secret police weare realized when the students began to chant slogans damning Lola Montez, and the rest of the crowd joined in.

Only a few uniformed constables were on duty in the streets on the line of march, and the secret police were reluctant to call on the army for support—principally because the crowd was good-natured and did not seem bent on destruction. All might have been well if Lola had not decided to take matters into her own hands.

Members of the Alemannia, who had not gone to Görres'

funeral, came to her house to tell her about the parade; she responded by going out into the street herself to confront the marchers. With the uniformed Alemannia acting as her escort, she came face to face with the opposition about four blocks from her villa.

The parade halted, the chants became louder, and the students in the front ranks unleashed a barrage of insults. Lola lost her temper and demanded that the marchers disband.

The conservative students refused.

Lola shouted, "Very well, I shall have the university closed!"

The youths in the student corps made a rush toward Lola, although what they would have done had they reached her side is not clear. The members of the Alemannia did not wait to find out; they formed a shield in front of her.

In minutes a first-class riot broke out. The secret police lacked the numbers to intervene, and so an immediate call was sent out for troops; but in the meantime the fighting grew worse. Swords were drawn, and one of the Alemannia leaders, young Count von Hirschenberg, was stabbed. When he collapsed onto the ground, blood spurting from the wound, he was believed dead. (His injuries proved to be superficial, and he recovered within a few days.)

The sight of the Count's blood convinced Lola that her own life was in danger, as perhaps it was, and she retreated across the street to the Church of the Theatines. The young conservatives were enraged by the realization that she had found safety in a Roman Catholic church, but they were reluctant to follow her there. Instead, they decided, they would lay siege to the church. Sooner or later, Lola would be forced to come out.

By this time two troops of cavalry and a full battalion of infantry had arrived on the scene. The officers in command of the troops did not want to fire into the crowd, and the students were ordered to return to the university. They defied the soldiers, holding their ground. The colonel in command finally ordered his mounted men to advance slowly with sabers drawn.

Threatened at sword point, the students slowly fell back, and the infantry moved in on their flanks. Seriously outnumbered by troops armed with muskets, the leaders of the corps agreed to disband. The students retired in good order to their dormitories.

A badly frightened Lola Montez went back to her villa, where she ordered a gift of fruit and flowers sent to Count von Hirschenberg, who had been taken to the hospital.

A short time later she was summoned to the palace for a conference with the King and his ministers that lasted for the rest of the day and far into the night. Lola insisted that the students be punished. The King agreed, and even the ministers were forced to admit that an important principle was at stake. If Ludwig's subjects could defy troops wearing the King's uniform, the rule of order would be placed in grave jeopardy.

There is no verification for the story that Lola wrote the decree published the following morning, or that she thrust a quill pen into the Elector's hand and demanded that he sign it. The unadorned facts are sufficiently dramatic: the university was closed, and all students who were not residents of the city were ordered to return to their homes within twenty-four hours.

Publication of the decree created an uproar. Most of the students were the sons of prominent citizens, who were dismayed by the prospect of their children's being denied a higher education. The merchants of the city were equally unhappy; the students, many of them wealthy, were among their best customers.

As for the students themselves, they marched in formation to the house of the university's rector and serenaded him for an hour; then the leader of each corps made a farewell speech. It is noteworthy that the Alemannia participated in this lugubrious ceremony, their differences with their foes forgotten in a time of joint crisis.

Meantime more than 2,000 citizens, many of them men of rank, stature, and wealth, were signing a petition begging the King to reconsider, to make allowances because the students were young and high-spirited. Among those who signed the document were Prince Wallerstein, whose son was a student, and four subministers, as well as an army major general and a number of colonels.

It was impossible for Ludwig to ignore such a request from some of the most important men in his realm. He retired to his study, where Lola Montez joined him that evening. Convinced it would be fatal for him to give in, she tried to convince him that the entire nation would regard any alteration of his firm stand as a sign of weakness.

Ludwig listened to Lola's advice, but on this occasion he failed to follow it. His principal desire at this point was the restoration of peace. It was said that Lola returned to her own little palace in the Barenstrasse, confident that Ludwig would accept her advice, and that she was shocked the next morning when he made his decision public.

The Royal Decree of February 10, 1848, in which Ludwig compromised by declaring that he would allow the university to reopen in three months, proved to be the disaster that Lola had feared. The opposition had scored a victory; the King was on the defensive. The shrewd politicians he had dismissed from office made the most of their opportunity.

It was no accident that a pamphlet written and published in Frankfort by Jacob Vennedey, a radical whose work had never appeared in Bavaria, suddenly flooded the country. It was the first direct attack on Ludwig himself his stunned subjects had ever seen, and as such it substituted spectacular charges for truth. It read, in part:

> The King of Bavaria wastes the resources of his poor land and the honest sweat of his honorable, persevering subjects on his mistresses and their depraved followers. Everyone knows that the jewelry Lola Montez wore recently at the theatre—and this is but a small portion of the collection given to her by the infatuated King—cost 60,000 guldens. Everyone knows that her house in the Barenstrasse is a fairy palace, that her bath alone cost 5,000 guldens, and that her paintings by great Masters are priceless.
>
> Everyone knows, too, that the Cabinet, the Council of State and the entire civil service are at her beck and call; that the police and the military are her particular escort, and that the principal function with which they are charged is the protection of her person.

Everyone knows that the best professors at the university have been dismissed at her caprice, her only reason being their Catholicism.

Because of this woman peaceful Bavaria has been transformed from a land of peace into a land of civil war and hate.

While this woman revels in her jewels, her fine paintings and her magnificent clothes, the King's loyal subjects plead in vain for a stable government and the chance to earn their living in peace and prosperity. But for the people nothing is done!

Bavaria will not recover from her illness until this woman is sent into exile, never to return!

If the King refuses to dismiss her, let him join her in exile! Let him also be sent in disgrace from the nation he has served so poorly!

Spurred by such propaganda, the populace finally decided that the situation had become intolerable. It is probably untrue that Karl von Abel and the senior members of the Jesuit hierarchy had a hand in the events that followed—there was no reason for them to intervene or otherwise make their influence felt. The facts are that the easygoing Bavarians had seen the peace of their nation disrupted, and they wanted no more.

On the morning of February 11, the members of the student corps, who had not gone off to their homes, marched on the palace. They were joined by so many thousands of citizens—men of every class, their wives, and even their children—that a full-scale revolution would have broken out had the troops been summoned from their barracks. Besides, as the top-ranking army officers made clear, they were not sure the soldiers would obey if ordered to disperse a throng that probably included members of their own immediate families.

The crowd had only one objective: to banish Lola Montez from Bavaria. "'Raus mit Lola!" The chant was taken up by thousands, but the King did not appear at the windows of the palace.

Had it been possible for Lola to join Ludwig at that critical hour, she might have strengthened his resolve. But there was no way she could make the short trip from the Barenstrasse to the palace. The streets were so clogged that no carriage could pass, and she would be in danger too great to risk, should she be recognized. Lola was forced to await developments under her own roof.

Government ministers went to the palace; when they were recognized, the crowd let them through. With the exception of Count von Berks, Lola had no real friends in the cabinet; all of its other members had tolerated her influence at best, and were heartily sick of being humiliated by a woman with no experience in government or politics. They added their voices to the clamor for her expulsion from the country, and Berks, who did not want to stand alone as Lola's champion, joined in the plea.

Former Prime Minister von Abel was passed through the crowd, as was the auxiliary Bishop of Munich. They, too, begged the King to dismiss his mistress, telling him it was his duty to make a personal sacrifice for the sake of restoring peace to his divided country. An hour or so before noon a deputation of Protestant leaders made its way through the still-growing crowd and gained admission to the palace. Ludwig saw them at once.

If he expected them to speak up on Lola's behalf, he was badly mistaken. These gentlemen realized, far better than anyone else, that the Lutherans of Bavaria would suffer if the King insisted on keeping Lola Montez in the country. Perhaps, if she left without further ado, they could consolidate the gains already achieved and not be made to suffer further hardships. And so they, too, petitioned Ludwig to submit.

The first news of importance was passed to the crowd just before noon, when Karl von Abel appeared at the main gate and asked the people to return to their homes. Members of Parliament, high-ranking nobles, and other officials were being summoned to a meeting at the Rathaus, and the King's decision would be made known to them. His Majesty, however, could not submit to threats.

Abel's broad smile told the people what they wanted to know. The crowd melted away; the students quietly marched back to their dormitories. Within a short time no more than a few hundred people stood in front of the palace, and only then was a cordon of troops stationed around the walls.

Before one o'clock in the afternoon, a mounted courier left the palace and rode to the Rathaus. Meanwhile Count von Rechberg, the aide-de-camp, slipped out a side door. The two men carried the same message, the courier taking the news to the leaders assembled at the Rathaus while Rechberg went to the little palace on the Barenstrasse. Both discharged their duties faithfully, reading aloud the brief decree just signed by Ludwig I.

It was His Royal Majesty's command that Lola Montez, Countess von Landsberg and Baroness von Rosenthal, depart from Bavaria forthwith.

[CHAPTER XVI]

There were no witnesses to the scene in Lola's private sitting room, so posterity has been forced to accept the claim of Count von Rechberg, who said she laughed, unbelieving, when he read King Ludwig's order expelling her from Bavaria. It is small wonder that Lola was incredulous: less than twenty-four hours had elapsed since she had last seen the King, and at their meeting he had indicated no change in his attitude toward her. Even his signature on the decree did not convince her, and she made no move until the singing and shouting of an approaching mob convinced her that the command had actually been issued. The citizens of Munich, celebrating their victory, were marching to her house to make certain the Elector's order was obeyed.

Lola snatched the strongbox that contained her jewels and a modest sum of cash, and, having informed Rechberg she would not leave the country until she saw the King in person, slipped out of the palace, wearing a hooded cloak over her gown. Trying to play for time, she took refuge for the second time in the Church of the Theatines.

Within minutes the mob reached her palace. When she failed to respond to calls to show herself, the crowd cut down two trees in front of the palace, intending to use the trunks as battering rams. Before the people could break in, King Ludwig appeared, accompanied only by a junior aide. The crowd parted to let him pass. A frightened servant opened the door for him, and he vanished inside.

A quarter of an hour later the King reappeared, bareheaded, pale, and obviously distraught. Those who stood nearest to him as he stalked to his mount heard him mutter, "She is gone, she is gone."

The secret police, who had cast their lot with the opposition, had been keeping a sharp watch for Lola at the railroad stations and on the roads leading from the city, and as no one had seen her, they conducted a thorough search in the vicinity of her palace. Eventually two agents found her in the Church of the Theatines. Uniformed reinforcements were summoned, and, when she refused to leave, she was carried bodily to a waiting coach and driven to the railroad station.

There a private car was attached to the train scheduled to leave for Berlin late in the afternoon. Once Lola had boarded it, a guard was placed around the car. A quarter of an hour before the train pulled out, Count von Rechberg arrived at the station, boarded the private car, spent a few minutes alone with Lola, then left.

A guard of troops accompanied Lola into the car as the train departed; she went straight to the ladies' rest room and locked the door behind her. Not until an hour and a half later, when the guards forced the door, did they discover that she had disappeared.

The train had made its usual suburban stop at the outer end of Nymphenburg Park, only three miles from the main station. There Lola had climbed out of the window on the side opposite the station, where a small carriage awaited her. She was driven, heavily veiled, to King Ludwig's private hunting lodge, Blüthenburg, located five miles from the city. Count von Rechberg had delivered the message: the King had arranged for her to hide at Blüthenburg, rightly believing no one would suspect she had taken refuge in a place so close to the capital.

Ludwig had intended to wait a few days, until the uproar died down, before going to the lodge, but he failed to take Lola's impatience into account. Having no intention of cowering like a fugitive behind the gates of the rustic lodge, she came up with a characteristically audacious scheme, which she carried out. Wearing an aide-de-camp's uniform she had found in a clothes closet at the lodge, she saddled one of the horses in the stable and rode into the city, going straight to the King's palace.

A full regiment of infantry, bayonets affixed to muskets, surrounded the royal compound. Lola, afraid she would be recognized if she tried to gain admittance, went instead to the home of her former champion, bachelor minister Count von Berks. He had no desire to become involved in Lola's scheme, but he had no choice, and at her insistence he sent a sealed note to the King.

There was no reply that night, which Lola spent at the house of Count Berks, but the next morning a royal courier arrived with a pass requesting the commandant of sentries to admit Count von Berks and one "Lieutenant von Reppel" to the palace. This order, signed by Ludwig, and his failure to grant her a pass in her own name, was Lola's first hint that the King might be more or less a prisoner in his own house.

She and Berks were passed through the sentry lines without incident, and Lola had a final meeting with the King behind the closed doors of his private study. Literally nothing is known about their conversation; Lola refused to discuss the subject or write about it, Ludwig himself kept quiet, and there were no witnesses. In the light of subsequent events, it is possible to deduce only that Ludwig must have convinced his mistress that he was powerless to do anything on her behalf.

According to a rumor that Lola confirmed in later years, Ludwig gave her the jewels she had not been able to take with her on her flight from Munich. They had been kept in a wall safe behind a painting in her bedchamber, and when the King had left her palace the day before, he took them with him. Although Ludwig could not prevent Lola's expulsion from Bavaria, she would not go penniless into the world.

Their private meeting was ended by the arrival of two high-ranking secret police officials who had been in charge of the search conducted for Lola ever since she had vanished from the train taking her into exile. One of them drew a pistol when he saw her. Lola—ever-impulsive, ever-intrepid—tried to snatch it from him. Ludwig prevented a fight by stepping between the principals.

Having no desire to implicate their sovereign as an accomplice in Lola's escape, the police agreed to smuggle her out of the country, thereby creating a bizarre situation: the secret police, charged with enforcing the King's decree, became his active partners in the partial circumvention of that order.

Apparently Ludwig hoped to hold another, longer meeting with Lola; perhaps to stay somewhere with her for several days before she actually left Bavaria. His secret police collaborators made their own plans accordingly, and Lola was smuggled out of Munich in a closed carriage with drawn drapes. The swift rush of events prevented Ludwig from joining her, and she did not see him again after they parted company in Munich.

Rumors circulated for years that Lola and her once-royal lover met secretly in Geneva, Paris, Madrid, and other cities. No evidence exists to prove the truth of these claims, and so it must be assumed that their meeting in Munich on a cold day in mid-February, 1848, was their last.

Little is known of Lola's precise whereabouts during the next two weeks, but she did spend several days at the estate of Baron Justinus von Kerner near the village of Weinsberg in rural Bavaria. Kerner, one of Ludwig's oldest and best friends, could be trusted to give refuge to a fugitive who would have been imprisoned, had her enemies captured her.

Kerner, whose correspondence with his daughter was published twenty-five years later, wrote that his guest was "a caged tiger." She ate virtually nothing and grew painfully thin. Unable to sit still, she paced the confines of his manor house; at night Kerner could hear her prowling around her room until daybreak. There can be no doubt that Lola suffered, although it is anyone's guess as to how much she mourned her loss of power and wealth and how much her parting from her royal benefactor-lover.

Ludwig had little opportunity to mourn the loss of Lola. During the next five weeks, the most difficult he had ever known, he learned that a ruler who shows his weakness can expect no mercy from those who want his power. The politicians demanded that he summon Parliament to a special session and give it increased authority. At first he refused, but finally he gave in and issued a decree summoning the legislators into session on March 16.

Men of all factions were demanding the resignation of Count von Berks, but Ludwig refused to dismiss him until the people rioted in the streets of Munich and other cities. He then gave in again and discharged Berks, but it was now too late to save himself. Virtually the entire nation joined in the attempt to persuade or force him to give up his throne; even his own younger brother, Prince Karl, was active in the movement. Catholics and Protestants stood together, nobles and commoners signed the same petitions, and when the principal army generals added their voices to the clamor, Ludwig realized he could hold out no longer. Armed mobs were marching through the streets of the capital, threatening to loot and burn, and the troops made no attempt to intervene.

And so, on March 21, 1848, the Elector Ludwig I signed his last royal decree:

Bavarians:
A new state of feeling has commenced—a state which differs essentially from that embodied in the constitution according to which I have governed this nation for twenty-three years. I abdicate my crown in favor of my beloved son, Crown Prince Maximilian, who succeeds me as Maximilian II.

My government has been in strict accordance with the constitution; my life has been dedicated to the welfare of my people. I have administered the public money and property as if I had been a republican officer, and I can boldly encounter the most severe scrutiny.

I offer my heartfelt thanks to all who have adhered to me faithfully, and although I descend from the throne of my ancestors, my heart still glows with affection for Bavaria and for Germany.

Long may Bavaria flourish, and long may her people thrive!

Ludwig

That afternoon a special train drew into the railroad station, and the royal household guard acted as an escort for a carriage in which two men were sitting. The younger, in full uniform, was King Maximilian II. Beside him was hunched a man who looked very old and tired in civilian clothes. Maximilian embraced his father, and Ludwig rode off into exile. No other members of the royal family were on hand to wish him godspeed.

The former monarch did not long remain a pitiful figure. Within a remarkably short time Ludwig regained his ebullience, and in less than a year he returned to one of the many private homes he still owned in Bavaria. Thereafter he spent the better part of his time at his various estates, refraining only from entering the capital. His interest in art never wavered, and in his retirement he purchased thirty-two paintings, twenty-six of which he presented as gifts to the people of Bavaria.

He survived his son and successor, Maximilian II, and witnessed the expulsion of a younger son, Otto, from the throne of Greece. Ludwig saw Prime Minister von Abel, restored to office, struggle in vain against the expansionist policies of Prince von Bismarck's Prussia, and he wept when Bavaria was incorporated into the greater Germany forged by the Prussians. He spent his declining years in Italy, whose works of art he so admired, traveling frequently to the south of France, where he maintained a villa overlooking the Mediterranean. Lola Montez was the last love of his life; he showed no subsequent interest in any other woman. He died at his villa in the hills outside Nice on February 29, 1868, in his eighty-third year, and the people of Munich subscribed to a fund to pay for the mammoth statue of him that was erected in Munich.

For a time it appeared that Lola Montez found life pleasant, too. She had escaped unharmed from Bavaria, she was wealthy, and she had a strongbox filled with cash and jewels. On March 2, 1848, she appeared at the Swiss border, accompanied by three students who were members of the Alemannia corps. How they happened to find her and join forces with her is unknown, but they remained at her side until she was safely settled in Bern.

Lola's arrival in Switzerland is appropriately described in her *Autobiography:*

> Her last hope for Bavaria being broken, she turned her attention toward Switzerland as the nearest shelter from the storm that was beating above her head. She had the previous year influenced the King of Bavaria to withhold his consent from a proposition by Austria, which had for its object the destruction of the little republic of Switzerland, and the Swiss people knew of her intervention on their behalf.
>
> If republics are ungrateful, Switzerland certainly was not so to Lola Montez; it received her with open arms, made her its official guest, and generously offered to bestow an establishment upon her for life.

For once Lola was not exaggerating. A furnished, fully staffed villa was placed at her disposal in the diplomatic quarter of Bern, the capital, and she was soon deluged with invitations to lunches, dinners, receptions, and teas given by Swiss officials and the various foreign legations. For as long as two months she declined to attend any function and spent most of her days riding alone, taking brisk walks through the streets of Bern, or reading in the drawing room of the villa.

According to rumors that would not be disproved for almost a century, Lola held a number of secret meetings with the exiled Ludwig during this period of her life. He had disappeared from sight after his train had crossed the Swiss border, and it was assumed by many, including certain newspapers in London and Paris, that he and Lola had been reunited.

Some portion of the mystery was explained late in World War II, when Allied bombers destroyed a building that had been erected in Munich soon after Ludwig's death. Someone, presumably a friend or relative of high station, had buried a packet of Lola Montez' letters to the deposed monarch, along with other of his private possessions, beneath the cornerstone of the building after his death; there they remained until a bomb dislodged them. These letters, all of them cheerful, all of them intended to raise Ludwig's spirits, were written over a period of several years, beginning in 1848, when she sent him an average of two communications a week. Ludwig had, of course, gone directly to Italy, but he and Lola wrote each other faithfully, even though they apparently did not abuse the hospitality of their host governments by meeting on foreign soil.

The letters were noteworthy more for their omissions than for what they said. Lola told her former protector that she was healthy, although a trifle lonely, and she recommended a number of books she wanted him to read. She herself had just finished reading Goethe's *Faust*, she told him in one letter, and found it far more powerful in the original German than in any other language. She described Swiss food, which she considered tasteless; and the weather, which she enjoyed. One could buy merchandise of any sort in the shops, where the clerks were remarkably polite; but prices were high, she said, so she resisted temptation.

Apparently Ludwig took the hint; for Lola, in her next letter, thanked him for his generous response. She mentioned no specific sum, but it was evident from her wording that he had sent her a sizable gift of cash. Ludwig had retained virtually all of his private fortune when he abdicated, and in later years, down to the last days of Lola's life, he invariably helped her when she asked him for funds. Whether or not they met again after their parting in Munich, Ludwig never lost his interest in the woman who had caused him to lose his throne.

When Lola began to pick up the threads of her social life, she faithfully reported details to Ludwig. She attended a reception at the legation of the new Republic of France, and there came face to face with Count Erich von Mittelheim, the Bavarian ambassador whom she had met in Munich when he had been a subminister in the cabinet of Prime Minister von Abel. Lola greeted him with mischievous pleasantry, behaving as though he were an old friend, and Mittelheim's embarrassment gratified her. He was forced by good manners to bend over her hand, she said, but the gesture was almost painfully brief. He stood red-faced for a moment or two, not knowing what to say to her, before he turned and plunged into the crowd, soon thereafter taking his leave.

The Swiss were clever diplomats, Lola wrote Ludwig, and were skilled in the art of protecting their small nation while not offending any of the great powers. The representatives of the new France were cultured gentlemen who knew nothing about diplomacy, and she believed them to be insufficiently alert to the possibility that the French monarchy might be restored. The French had been accustomed to the rule of kings for too long to change their habits now, and she predicted that the republic would survive for only a short time—a prophecy that came to pass a few years later, when President Louis Napoleon Bonaparte made himself Napoleon III.

The Prussians, Lola wrote, were insufferably arrogant, and could talk of nothing but the expansion that was Prince von Bismarck's aim. Bavaria could not remain independent without strong alliances, and she feared that Prime Minister von Abel was not far-sighted enough to make such treaties. The Austrians were charming, devious, and ever-conscious of their high place as representatives of the most powerful nation on the Continent. The Russians were reserved, addressed no one but each other at diplomatic functions, and seemed suspicious of anyone who tried to strike up friendly conversations with them. She made no mention of her supposed fellow countrymen, although Spain maintained one of the largest legations in Bern.

Lola reserved her most glowing compliments for the English. Not only were the members of the English legation sophisticated and able to converse on any subject. but they were masters of the arts of diplomacy, representing the interests of their queen and country brilliantly. They served the most lavish dinners in Bern, their chef was an artist, even their punch was colder than that served at any other legation. It was a joy to dine there and participate in the stimulating conversation. Everyone looked up to the English, even though they held themselves somewhat aloof, and it was they who set the pace and established the tone of the diplomatic community.

Had Ludwig known of Lola's origins, he would have recognized her enthusiasm for the English and their ways as chauvinism. But he had believed his mistress to be of Spanish descent up to the time of her departure from Munich, and there is nothing in her correspondence with him indicating that she later revealed the truth to him.

In any case, something more than chauvinism was responsible for Lola's praise. An Englishman had appeared on her horizons, and she delicately refrained from mentioning him in her letters to Ludwig.

[CHAPTER XVII]

Robert Peel, the handsome British chargé d'affaires in Bern, was the brilliant son of an even more brilliant father, Sir Robert Peel, leader of the Conservative party and former Prime Minister. Like his father, whose reforms had won him enormous popularity among the middle and lower classes as well as in the ranks of the aristocracy, the younger Peel was a humanitarian devoted to the cause of expanding personal liberties.

So it is not strange that he should have been drawn to the thirty-year-old beauty who, according to the liberal press of the world, had lost her place and her fortune in Bavaria because she had been the champion of freedom and had fought for it without regard for herself.

Little has come to light about Lola's relationship with Peel, whom she mentions only briefly in her *Autobiography* and elsewhere as a friend. Any correspondence they may have exchanged has been lost, and both principals seemed reluctant to discuss each other. Bern gossiped about them, to be sure, but not every man whose name was linked with Lola's was her lover.

In any event, it was Peel who ended her self-imposed isolation. He shared Lola's enjoyment of an early-morning canter, and the two were often seen together on the bridle paths a short time after sunrise. They began to have lunch together on occasion, and it was not long before the British chargé d'affaires became Lola's escort at the diplomatic functions she had previously avoided.

The curious—that is to say, the entire diplomatic set and most Swiss officials—were eager to listen to her, and no one was more sought after than Lola during the summer and autumn of 1848. She gradually recovered her sharp sense of humor, and she spoke with facility on many subjects, but it was noted that she avoided any mention of King Ludwig or of the role she had played in Bavarian politics. The less discreet sometimes tried to question her about her life in Munich, but she invariably replied with a cold stare and, if her inquisitor persisted, turned her attention elsewhere.

Lola's stay in Bern was a necessary interlude while she regained her energy, and it may be that Peel also helped restore her self-confidence. By the time winter came, she was restless again, finding life in Switzerland too dull to suit her. Peel, in one of the few comments about her attributed to him, is alleged to have said, "Lola could never be content basking in the fading glow of her Bavarian experience. She resembled Alexander the Great, and had a real need for fresh worlds to conquer."

In mid-December of 1848, Lola gave up her villa and disappeared from Bern. If she and Ludwig ever enjoyed a reunion, it must have taken place during the weeks that followed; nothing is known of her whereabouts during this period. But had she visited Ludwig in Rome, where he was spending the winter, the penny press presumably would have discovered the fact and trumpeted the news.

Lola made a sudden reappearance in London in early January of 1849, taking lodgings in Half Moon Street, Piccadilly, then one of the most fashionable and expensive residential neighborhoods in the city. Since her lack of sentimentality precludes the possibility that she was homesick, why she elected to return to England is something of a mystery. Certainly her judgment was poor. There were many in society, the theater, and military circles who were familiar with her background and identity, and she could hardly have forgotten the circumstances under which she had left the country. Perhaps she felt that the stature and relative wealth she had gained since her departure would mock those who had jeered at her.

Lola's Piccadilly quarters were spacious, ten rooms on two floors; and she quickly hired a cook, a maid of all work, and a personal maid. Word of her arrival spread slowly, but within a month gentlemen were calling on her at receptions she held during the early evening hours. One of them, the Hon. F. Leveson Gower, said in his *Bygone Years,* published more than fifty years later: "She had lost none of her good looks, and her animated conversation was entertaining." Another, George Augustus Sala, then a young writer who was to enjoy a distinguished career as a journalist, later revealed in his *Life and Adventures of* G. A. *Sala* that he and Lola discussed the possibility that he might write her biography.

She told him she was the daughter of Montes, the greatest of Spanish bullfighters, who had taught her his craft when she was a small child. Only the prejudices of society against the sight of a woman in the bull ring had prevented her from following her father's vocation. Their business deal fell through, Sala wrote, because Lola demanded such a large percentage of the author's royalties that the project would not have paid him enough to be worth his time and effort.

Another of Lola's acquaintances at this time was Lord Brougham, currently the Lord Chancellor and a man whose humanitarian liberalism had won him a wide following. He created something of a sensation one day in late February of 1849 when he escorted Lola to the Peeresses' Gallery at the House of Lords, where she then heard him taking part in a debate. This may have been Lola's way of servnig notice on her former detractors that she still held two Bavarian titles and therefore was entitled to sit in the gallery reserved for noblewomen.

By now Lola was beginning to show familiar signs of restlessness. The directors of Covent Garden came to her with the extraordinary idea that she star in a drama in which she would play herself. The work, to be called *Lola Montez, Countess for an*

Hour, would dramatize her life in Bavaria. Lola would have full censorship rights, the script being prepared under her direction. She was offered such a large sum of money to participate in the venture that she abandoned the scruples she had shown in Bern and indicated her willingness to appear in the autobiographical play.

But the office of the Lord Chamberlain had censorship rights greater than Lola's, and when Covent Garden applied for a license to present the play, the license was refused. The Lord Chamberlain ruled that it would be indiscreet to present living royalty on the stage, and it was rumored in theatrical circles that Queen Victoria was pleased by the decision.

Lola now had no choice but to keep up her social life, and she must have realized that she was not acceptable in the higher circles. Her affair with Ludwig, combined with her previously publicized liaisons with Liszt and Dujarier, had placed her beyond the pale. No ladies visited her salon, and any married man who dropped in from time to time for conversation and a glass of sherry kept quiet about it. Most of her visitors were bachelors.

Frozen out by the people she most wanted to impress, Lola again showed her naïveté in judging conventions. A more sophisticated woman in her position would have realized from the outset how many doors were permanently closed to her. But one of Lola's most glaring weaknesses was her lack of perspective.

Having returned to a nation that prized respectability, she decided she would achieve acceptance by making a good marriage. She conveniently forgot that under English law she was still a married woman, her husband having been granted a separation that prevented either party from remarrying.

Lola was not one to let such details stand in her way. The man she selected as her new mate was George Trafford Heald, the son of a wealthy and influential barrister, who held a lieutenant's commission in the Second Life Guards. Heald, who was ten years Lola's junior, had a number of qualities that attracted her: he was tall and good-looking; he rode a horse magnificently; and, when he celebrated his twenty-first birthday a few months earlier, he had come into an income of £10,000 per year, the equivalent of $100,000 in modern times.

Not surprisingly, Heald was regarded as one of the most eligible bachelors in London. Determined mothers pursuing him on behalf of their daughters must have been dismayed when Heald began to be seen at the theater and in restaurants with Lola Montez, but they undoubtedly consoled themselves with the thought that he was merely enjoying the fling that was recognized as his privilege before he found the right young lady and settled into his proper place in an ordered world.

Apparently it occurred to no one that Heald had fallen in love with Lola—if indeed he had, and was not simply dazzled by her. What she actually thought of him is equally difficult to determine, although most of her nineteenth-century biographers gallantly gave her the benefit of their very natural doubts. Regardless of her real feelings, Lola had no difficulty in persuading Heald that she loved him, and that was what counted.

On July 19, 1849, Miss Lola Montez and Mr. George T. Heald were married at St. George's Church, Hanover Square, with the unsuspecting rector officiating. The happy couple went off to Scotland for a brief honeymoon—surely Heald's choice, considering Lola's experiences there as a child.

If she thought her days as Betty James were forgotten, Lola discovered the magnitude of her mistake soon after she and Heald returned to London on August 3 to take up residence at the Half Moon Street address. At nine o'clock on the morning of August 6, the new Mrs. Heald emerged from her house and started across the walk toward her carriage, which was waiting to take her shopping. Two solidly built men in mufti approached and, after ascertaining her identity, introduced themselves as Inspector Whall and Police Sergeant Gray of Scotland Yard. They deeply regretted the necessity of informing her that she was under arrest, charged with bigamy.

Lola's response was as imaginative as it was heated. According to the official report submitted by Inspector Whall to his superiors, she claimed that Scotland Yard's records were mistaken and that she had been divorced from Captain James by a special Act of Parliament. She also informed him: "I don't know whether Captain James is still alive, and I don't care. I was married under a false name, so it wasn't a legal marriage. Lord Brougham was present when my divorce was granted, and Captain Osborne (Heald's commanding officer, later Lord Osborne) can also prove it."

The two officers felt it necessary to take her off to the nearest police station and book her. As they climbed in beside her, Lola murmured, "What will the King think?" One presumes she was referring to her protector, Ludwig, late of Bavaria.

A hearing was held that same afternoon at the Marlborough Street Police Court, Magistrate Peregrine Bingham presiding. The London *Times* of August 7 described the scene warmly:

At half past one o'clock the Countess of Landsberg (sic), leaning on the arm of Mr. Heald, her present husband, came into the court and was accommodated with a seat in front of the bar. Mr. Heald was also allowed to have a chair beside her.

The lady appeared quite without embarrassment, and smiled several times as she made remarks to her husband. She was stated to be 24 years of age on the police-sheet, but has the look of a woman a trifle older. She was dressed in black silk, with close-fitting black velvet jacket, a plain white straw bonnet trimmed with blue, and blue veil. She is full of figure, but has a very small waist, of pale-dark complexion, the lower part of the features symmetrical, the upper part less so, owing to rather prominent cheekbones, but set off by a pair of unusually large blue eyes with long, black lashes.

Her reputed husband, Mr. Heald, during the whole of the proceedings, sat with the Countess' hand clasped in both of his own, occasionally giving it a fervent squeeze, and at particular parts of the evidence whispering to her with the fondest air, and pressing her hand to his lips with great warmth.

The prosecutor, a Mr. Clarkson, opened his case by revealing to the court the name of the complainant in the case: Miss Susanna Heald, George's aunt, who felt she owed it to the memory of her late brother to intervene. Clarkson cited the legal facts of Lola's first marriage and legal separation, and then introduced incontrovertible evidence into the record to the effect that Major Thomas James had been alive, in India, thirty-six days earlier. He proposed that Lola be remanded until additional evidence could be obtained, either in person or by deposition, from witnesses currently living in India.

Miss Heald went into the witness box, where she stated that she had been George's guardian for two years prior to his coming of age and that she had felt it her duty to continue to protect the young man. Having learned of the marriage a month before it took place, she had instituted inquiries at that time. Although she gleaned enough information in time to prevent the wedding, she had not been able to believe that Heald's intentions were serious. Wiser now, she was acting in the hope that the ceremony would be invalidated. The court ordered her to step down when she claimed that Lola was a money-hungry woman who was interested in her nephew only because of his inheritance.

Lola did not take the stand in her own defense. She was represented by a barrister, a Mr. Bodkin, who apologized to the court for his lack of preparation and explained that he had been retained only two hours earlier. After stating that Lola had been married as a child, when she had not known what she was doing, he expressed his own certainty that a divorce had taken place. His client, he said, was under the strong impression that a divorce bill had been obtained in the House of Lords. He admitted the possibility that his client might be mistaken, but insisted that, in this event, she was not guilty of deliberate falsehood but was merely ignorant of British laws.

Bodkin requested that the court set Lola free on bail pending the gathering of evidence from sources in India and elsewhere, and assured Magistrate Bingham that his client, who was anxious to obtain justice, had only one desire, that of clearing her good name at the first opportunity.

Magistrate Bingham said that the facts as presented made it unlikely that additional evidence could alter the circumstances of the defendant. He did admit the remote possibility that Major

James might have been killed in action during recent skirmishes in India, and there was even a chance that he might have been carried away by cholera. In any case the court demanded proof beyond the word of Miss Heald and her barrister to the effect that the defendant's first husband was still alive.

Pending the receipt of that proof, Bingham said, he would set the defendant free when she posted a bail of £2,000. The size of the bail, far higher than the amount usually set, suggests that the court was convinced that Lola was guilty. But Magistrate Bingham was kind enough to grant Lola and Heald the right to remain in the courtroom until the capacity crowd that had gathered to hear the case was dispersed.

Bodkin conferred briefly with Lola, at which time she told him she did not doubt Susanna Heald's ability to obtain a deposition from Major James. The old lady was such a dragon, Lola said, that she would not be surprised if she managed to bring James back to England and produce him in person at the trial.

Shortly before dawn the following morning, a carriage pulled away from 27 Half Moon Street, followed by a cart piled high with leather traveling boxes. In the back of the coach were a veiled woman and a man with a broad-brimmed hat pulled low over his face. On the morning of August 8, the *Herald* informed its readers that Lola Montez and George Heald had forfeited the bond by departing secretly from England, via Folkestone and Boulogne, for an undisclosed destination on the Continent.

[CHAPTER XVIII]

Nineteenth-century Boulogne was the fishing capital of France and was enjoying a spectacular growth as a commercial shipping center, but it provided few facilities for luxury-minded travelers. There were no hotels in the little city worthy of the name, so George Heald found it necessary to engage a small suite in a rooming house for himself and the woman he considered his bride.

Lola, more experienced, encountered no difficulty in establishing the two of them on the scale to which her recent life had accustomed her. The only restaurant in town that served food she thought fit for her palate was the Austerlitz, named in honor of one of the Emperor Napoleon's greatest victories, and for the next week she and Heald dined there every night. Her unerring instinct also led her to the emporium of the one jeweler in Boulogne whose merchandise was comparable to that sold in the finest London and Paris shops. The proprietor later revealed to a British newspaper reporter that she had spent two afternoons carefully examining his wares, and then returned again with a handsome young English gentleman in tow. She showed him a ring she had selected, and he happily paid £1,500 for it.

The charm of Boulogne having worn thin, the half-married honeymooners departed, twenty-four hours before reporters picked up their trail. It was not until several years later that she revealed they had paid a visit to Paris under assumed names. Heald engaged a suite at the King William Hotel, the fashionable hostelry patronized by their wealthier compatriots, and Lola showed her bemused young lover the Paris with which she had become only slightly acquainted when living there as Dujarier's mistress. They made the rounds of the jewelers and perfumers, and a dressmaker spent several hours at the suite each day as Lola busied herself with fittings for the new wardrobe she was having made.

Then, the piles of leather traveling boxes having grown appreciably, the couple went on to Spain, which the ingenuous Heald still believed to be his bride's native land. Perhaps he was even more naïve than he appeared; it is nonetheless a tribute to Lola's talents that she could convince him—so soon after testimony to the contrary in the London police court—that she was of Spanish descent.

After a brief visit to Madrid, Toledo, and several other cities, the fugitive honeymooners settled in a hotel suite in Barcelona for a protracted stay. It was there that Heald first began to realize the woman in his life might not be the wronged angel he imagined her to be. In spite of the luxuries he lavished on Lola, she was bored and was showing the strain of spending all her waking hours in the company of an intellectual inferior. The men in whom her interest had been genuine—Liszt, Dujarier, and King Ludwig—had been out of the ordinary, but all she found genuinely appealing about Heald was his money. She quarreled with him, occasionally giving way to magnificent fits of temper, and the newspaper reporters who had discovered the couple's presence in Barcelona informed their London and Paris readers that the young man seemed bewildered.

During this period the London *Herald* started referring to Lola as the Countess of Landsfeld, not Landsberg; the author of the articles was obviously unaware that there was no Landsfeld in Bavaria. Other newspapers copied the *Herald's* error, but Lola made no attempt to call the attention of editors to the mistake. Instead, she accepted the new name, and for the rest of her life called herself the Countess of Landsfeld whenever the press used the name. Her precise title apparently was of no significance to her; all that mattered was the right to call herself a countess.

According to Eugene de Miracourt, whose book *Les Contemporains* was published in Paris soon after Lola's death, her relations with Heald deteriorated so rapidly during the couple's Barcelona sojourn that she slashed him on the arms and chest with the small double-edged knife she had taken to carrying at all times. The injuries, painful but not serious, left permanent scars. Heald, more confused than ever and not knowing where else to turn, went to the British consul in Barcelona for advice. Whatever the embarrassed consul may have been tempted to say, he merely informed Heald that the matter was beyond the scope of his official competence.

Contemporary press sources corroborate the separation of Lola and Heald in Barcelona. It appears that she definitely left their suite there, taking her luggage with her, and went back to Madrid. It must have been evident to Lola by this time that this pseudo-marriage could offer her no permanent shelter, and she began in earnest to prepare for a resumption of the career she had abandoned in Bavaria. She rented a small apartment in a fashionable residential quarter, and soon the press was reporting that Lola was attending the theater, alone, or going to cafés, heavily veiled, and watching the performances of entertainers there. It did not occur to the reporters that she was studying the work of Spanish dancers in order to improve the techniques that critics of so many cities had branded as incomparably bad.

If Lola assumed that George Heald had disappeared permanently from her life, she was mistaken; he was more of a glutton for punishment than any reasonable person could have imagined. He had stayed on in Barcelona, sulking, after Lola left, and when he read in the newspapers that she had gone to Madrid, he followed her there to beg for a reconciliation.

Lola graciously allowed him to pay her rent for a period of six months and, upon the presentation of new jewels, including a gold necklace set with rubies and other gems, permitted him to move into her apartment. The incompatibility that had caused their initial break was, of course, unchanged, and Lola treated Heald with such contempt that he was forced to run from her again, this time all the way to England.

She wrote his epitaph in the form of a small advertisement placed in the Madrid newspapers: a puppy had been lost, and she was offering a reward to anyone who found the animal and returned him to his owner. Madrid was amused, and Madrid's bachelors took Lola's hint to the effect that she would be willing to accept invitations to dinner and the theater.

Meanwhile the disillusioned Heald found that his infatuation and marriage had ruined his life. He had been discharged from the Royal Army on a technical charge, the mothers of eligible daughters looked down their patrician noses at him, and—worse—gentlemen laughed at him whenever he appeared in public. Under his aunt's guidance he tried to begin anew, his first step being to apply for an annulment of his marriage. The court ruled that his request could not be granted since the marriage ceremony had not been legal, which left Heald with the somewhat dubious satisfaction of knowing that his bachelor status was officially recognized.

Unable to tolerate the ostracism he felt on every side, he moved from England to Portugal, returning briefly to spend the Christmas holidays with his aunt. His short life came to a sudden tragic end the following summer, when a small boat in which he was sailing capsized within sight of shore and he was drowned.

Lola was advised of Heald's fortunes only through what she read in the newspapers. After his court appearance she never again referred to herself as Mrs. Heald, but once again became Lola Montez, Countess of Landsberg or of Landsfeld, depending on what name the local press was using. Her reputation, particularly in England, was more tarnished than ever, but her collection of jewelry had grown, as had her wardrobe, and Lola counted her blessings.

It was not long before she realized how much harm the Heald incident had done her. She had the sense not to seek work in Madrid, but her life there became uncomfortable nonetheless. The ladies snubbed her, and the gentlemen wanted more than her companionship at dinner or the theater. Having no intention of staying on in Spain as a high-priced courtesan, she returned to Paris in the hope that she could resume her theatrical work there.

France had changed since Lola's last sojourn there. There were rumors that the President of the Second Republic, Prince Louis Napoleon Bonaparte, planned to make himself a dictator, and everyone in literary and artistic circles seemed preoccupied with politics. Old acquaintances avoided Lola, theater managers turned down her requests for employment; no one, it seemed, had much time for frivolity. Men continued to take mistresses, to be sure, and Lola at thirty-one was still a beauty, but she apparently refused a number of offers. In her own eyes, if nobody else's, she was a woman of stature, an internationally recognized celebrity, a member of the Bavarian nobility.

Then, too, she had no need for money. She had spent almost none of her comfortable nest egg, so it may be that Ludwig was still sending her money from Italy and the south of France.

Despite her freedom from financial worries, Lola was desperately unhappy. She was no longer in the limelight. Theater owners had no interest in hiring her. The Paris press took no interest in her movements, and even the gossips of the penny press were devoting so much space to politics that her name was rarely mentioned in print, no matter how distinguished her dinner escort might be.

Deprived of a stage, Lola became increasingly restless and, after several remarkably uneventful months in Paris, made up her mind to brave the scorn of her compatriots and return to London. There the same fate awaited her; the newspapers, which previously had printed column after column about her, made no mention of her arrival. She took lodgings in Half Moon Street again and, apparently in no way discouraged by the silence of the press, sent notes to inform friends and acquaintances that she was in town.

A new series of shocks awaited her. Even as Dumas and Gautier had been too busy to see her in Paris, so the men she had known in England took pains to avoid her. Lord Brougham made no reply to her note, a slight that inspired withering comments about him in her *Autobiography*. Other gentlemen were equally cavalier in their treatment of her, and Lola either did not know or could not face the reason: their own reputations would be seriously damaged should they call on her or allow themselves to be seen with her in public.

In short, the Heald affair had been too much for an England that demanded at least a surface observance of convention. Lola Montez was no longer the liberal heroine who had been forced to flee from Bavaria after fighting for individual freedoms in that repressed country. Beautiful she might be, but the people of the British Isles universally regarded her as an adventuress so notorious that no self-respecting person dared be seen in her company.

In the autumn of 1850, Lola made increasingly frantic efforts to break down the barriers that excluded her from the society of honorable Englishmen. The most renowned of English actors, Charles John Kean, son of the great Edmund Kean, was scheduled to appear with his wife, Ellen, in a command performance of *Macbeth* at the Princess Theatre. Everyone of consequence would be present—it was even said that Queen Victoria and Prince Albert, who had recently celebrated the birth of their seventh child, would make one of their rare public appearances.

How Lola managed to buy a box for the evening when seats were in such demand is a secret, but few things lay beyond her grasp when she wanted them badly enough. Unfortunately her taste and her sense of decorum were less well developed than her ambition.

According to a custom dating from the reign of James I, ticket-holders made it their business to be in their seats before their monarch arrived. Hundreds of Victoria's loyal subjects dutifully observed the convention and stood as the Queen and her consort entered the royal box. Only a few sharp-eyed members of the audience noticed that the box opposite Victoria's was as yet unoccupied.

The patrons applauded, Victoria and Albert bowed, and the management waited a few moments for people to settle in their seats before dimming the house lights and raising the curtain. It was during this minute or two that the Princess Theatre's audience was electrified by the late appearance of a radiantly lovely woman, a diamond tiara blazing above the crown of her auburn hair, a long cloak of ermine, the fur of royalty, falling from her shoulders. Even Victoria and Albert stared at the box on the opposite side of the theater as the young woman dropped her cloak to reveal a bare-armed, low-necked gown of crimson velvet. Members of the audience were still whispering as the curtain rose and they shifted their attention to Shakespeare's Weird Sisters.

Quite apart from her rudeness in making an appearance after the Queen's arrival, Lola's choice of color for her gown could not have been more unfortunate. Streetwalkers of London and major Continental cities advertised their wares by wearing red; Lola had made obvious comparisons inevitable. Members of the audience turned toward the royal box in time to see a lady-in-waiting whisper a few words to the Queen and the Prince Consort, who took care not to glance again in the direction of the lady in crimson.

If Lola had hoped to bring herself to the attention of London society so dramatically that no one could ignore her, she succeeded —for a moment. The aristocratic audience then followed the Queen's example by looking in every direction except Lola's; the actors in the audience, annoyed by what they regarded as a deliberate insult to Charles Kean, followed suit.

The debacle at the Princess Theatre produced other, more serious effects. Lola's ostracization was now so complete that not even the most newly rich manufacturer could so much as appear to recognize her in public. As a consequence Lola had literally nothing with which to occupy her time; so she sat down to write what would become the first version of her *Autobiography*. The book was destined to become one of the biggest sellers of the age, and Lola would prepare two later editions, bringing readers up to date.

Although Lola had never written anything of consequence, her *Autobiography* was a logical step forward at this time. Her ego demanded that she remain in the public eye, and all other doors were closed to her. There was a ready market for the memoirs of a notorious international adventuress who had been the mistress of a king, and when Lola sent word to the publishers of Paris that she was working on an autobiography, four or five of them bid for it.

She held out for such high terms that only one publisher, Georges Lefèvre, was willing to meet her demands. He subsequently went bankrupt, but it is not known whether Lola's book contributed to his plight.

One of the odder aspects of her new career as an author was that she wrote her book in English, then translated it herself into French. Knowing there would be requests for it from publishers in the English-speaking world after the French edition was published, she kept the original, which was ready for printing when London publishers approached her.

The rich man and the aristocrat who could neither call on Lola nor be seen in public with her could buy the book and read it in the privacy of their own homes. They did, and Lola's dramatization of her life sold enough copies to guarantee her a substantial income for many years. As Lola herself was well aware, the book also guaranteed that she would remain in the public eye.

The snubs of London and Paris served yet another purpose, inspiring Lola to turn away from the Old World that no longer appreciated her. Gold had been discovered in distant California two years earlier, and the adventuress, like so many others, dreamed of the opportunities of the New World. One of thousands who invested in a gold-mining company, Lola was more fortunate than most of her contemporaries, who poured hundreds of thouhands of pounds into ventures that failed overnight. She invested £3,000 in the stock of the famous Eureka Mining Company. In her last years she would boast that she had known from the outset that gold would be found in abundance on the property belonging to Eureka.

Lola's gold stock accomplished more than repaying her at a rate of better than seven to one: it focused her attention on the New World, at which point it occurred to her that the United States was a wealthy, growing nation that she had not yet conquered.

[CHAPTER XIX]

On November 20, 1851, putting behind her the homeland that had so coldly rejected her, Lola Montez traveled from London to Southampton and there boarded the pride of the American merchant marine, the coal-burning transatlantic steamship *Humboldt*. The accommodations on power-driven vessels were less luxurious than those on clipper ships, but steamers were more reliable, maintaining their schedules and offering passengers a smoother passage.

The *Humboldt* boasted two salons, a dining room, and a smoking room, as well as private cabins on her upper decks, one of which Lola occupied. She was accompanied only by a personal maid, who had quarters below. A fellow passenger was Louis Kossuth, the fiery editor who had led the unsuccessful Hungarian insurrection of 1848–49 and had escaped into exile after troops of the mighty Austro-Hungarian Empire had crushed his rebellion. Famous as one of the world's leading liberals, Kossuth presumably had much in common with Lola, but their paths did not cross until the final days of the voyage. Kossuth spent the better part of the trip in bed, seasick; by the time he recovered, Lola had become friendly with a wealthy New Yorker, Samuel D. Chambers, a manufacturer of locomotives who owned plants in a number of American cities. Lola and Kossuth dined at the same table, but she had no interest in a political refugee. A wealthy American industrialist, however, was fair game.

Demonstrating to her own satisfaction that she had not lost her talent for finding and charming a man who could offer her the greatest assistance when she needed it, Lola struck up a relationship with Chambers that was unique in her experience. He was a widower in his sixties, traveling with his son and daughter-in-law, and Lola's instinct told her not to flirt with him. Apparently Chambers became her friend rather than her lover. His son and daughter-in-law treated her pleasantly, too, the latter regarding her as an equal and giving her some insight into the differences between Old and New World society.

By the time the *Humboldt* steamed past the Battery on December 5 and made her way up the Hudson River to her Manhattan berth, Chambers had promised to give Lola any financial backing she might need, should she decide to appear on the stage as an actress or dancer. It is small wonder that she was scarcely aware of Louis Kossuth's presence.

The reporters who had boarded the steamer at quarantine paid far more attention to Lola than to the Hungarian patriot. Enjoying her first experience of an American press conference, she answered impertinent, breezy questions in kind, meeting frankness with frankness.

The interview published on December 6, 1851, by the New York *Tribune* was typical. The writer expressed surprise at Lola's appearance, having been led by her exploits to believe she might resemble an Amazon. Instead, he declared, she was of slender, almost delicate build, her figure that of a girl in her teens. Her nose was Grecian, and her cheekbones were so high that they gave her face a Moorish cast. He judged Lola to be in her twenties, an observation for which she thanked him · How, he inquired, had she kept so slim?

She was careful of what she ate, Lola replied, rarely touching bread and never being tempted by puddings or cakes.

What were her views of America?

She laughed, reminding the press that she had not yet set foot on American soil. She was, however, afraid that the United States had already formed its opinions of her, and she could only hope she was mistaken. If it was true that the country had made up its mind about her, the press was to blame because so many falsehoods had been printed.

One of the reporters asked her for an example.

"All right," she said. "I am reputed to be a bad woman. But I will tell you something confidential. If I were only a fraction as wicked as I am reputed to be, I am sure I would have many times the number of admirers I actually have."

She sounded, one of the newsmen said, as though she did not have much faith in men.

"Do you know any reason I should have faith in them?" Lola responded.

After the laughter subsided, someone remarked that she must have met a number of American men over the years.

She admitted that she had.

Predictably the reporter asked her opinion of American males as opposed to Englishmen and Europeans.

Lola avoided his trap. All men were identical in their desires, she declared, but Americans were far more honest in telling a pretty, single woman what they wanted.

Did she deliberately enslave men?

"I do not believe in slavery of any kind," she replied, thereby stepping into the most bitter of American controversies. Her response was widely quoted by the Abolitionists of the North, but the slave-owning states of the South were not offended, presumably because they assumed she was giving a light answer to an impertinent question. Within a few months Lola had proved she was in earnest by purchasing a young slave as a maidservant and immediately granting the girl her freedom, while retaining her as an employee on generous salary.

Did she intend to confine her visit to New York?

"I do not, sir," she said. "I hope to visit many of your cities, provided they will give me a friendly reception."

America, a reporter insisted, was known for its hospitality; he could not understand Miss Montez' comment.

This gave Lola a chance to reveal her plans. She had not come to the United States on a sight-seeing holiday but as a professional woman who had to work in order to earn a living. She planned to make a series of stage appearances as an actress and as a dancer, performing in some of the vehicles that had delighted the crowned heads of so many European nations.

However, she continued, as the reporters and many American newspaper readers well knew, the press of Europe had been unkind to her on more than one occasion. This was not the appropriate time to rake up the past, although it would be easy enough to explain why so many critics had hated her. Then, scarcely pausing for breath, she hinted that it was the custom in the European theater for reviewers to expect favors from those women performers whom they praised in print and that her own personal standards had made it impossible for her to grant such favors.

All she asked of New York and other American cities, Lola said, was that discriminating audiences make their judgment solely on the basis of her stage performances. If they refrained from prejudging her, she could ask nothing more; she was not concerned, because she had complete faith in the fairness of the American people.

She was prepared, too, for the inevitable questions about King Ludwig and Dujarier. Had she been the mistress of either?

"I was Ludwig's political adviser and Dujarier's friend. Would I be forced to earn my living on the stage if I had been the mistress of such wealthy men as these?"

She refused to be quoted on only one subject, her so-called marriage to George Heald. "I never discuss personal matters," she said.

The interview was so successful that the reporters procured a carriage for her and several of them insisted on escorting her to the Howard Hotel. There a suite, a pet spaniel, and her lady's maid awaited her.

Once the press had trumpeted the news of Lola's arrival, she was besieged by callers, the New York *Post* reporting that on December 6 alone, more than fifty gentlemen left their cards at the desk of the hotel. None were admitted to the suite, however; Lola was playing a careful game. On December 7 her shipboard friend Samuel Chambers gave a dinner party in her honor, and only the ladies and gentlemen she met there were allowed to call on her in the days that followed. There was a strong streak of Puritanism in America, as Lola well knew, and she had no intention of offending her future public through behavior that might outrage their standards.

One man whom she had not met socially gained entrance to Lola's suite without being sent away or being forced to write her a long explanation of his mission. He was Edward Willis, one of the shrewdest and most successful theatrical managers in the United States, who had a far greater reputation in intellectual circles than his rival, P. T. Barnum. Both Willis and Barnum had written to Lola in England, offering her American engagements, and she preferred to be associated with Willis. In the United States, if nowhere else, she was going to be treated in a dignified manner suitable to the Countess of Landsberg—or Landsfeld.

Lola struck a hard bargain with Willis. Inasmuch as she had obtained the financial support of Chambers, she demanded more than a salary from Willis, insisting that he split 80 percent of the profits with her and repay her backer out of the remaining 20 percent. Edward Willis agreed.

Lola carried, in one of her traveling boxes, the script and score of a musical comedy called *Betley the Tyrolean,* which she claimed had been written for her. As the names of no author, composer, or lyricist ever appeared in print in connection with the play, some theatrical historians have assumed that Lola wrote the entire work herself. The script was weak, the music anything but memorable, and the lyrics insipid, but Willis reasoned that there were so many theatergoers in New York who wanted to see Lola Montez that the vehicle was not important.

Betley went into rehearsal on December 12, just five days after Lola's arrival, and opened at the Broadway Theatre on December 27. In spite of the care she had taken to behave like a lady, there were only a few women in the opening night audience. Her male admirers applauded vigorously as Lola recited lines, danced, and sang in a vaudeville potpourri, and her success seemed assured. The following day when the newspaper critics rendered their verdict, Lola's faith in the American male was justified. The reviewers commented at length and in glowing terms on her physical attributes, the *Tribune* calling her "the most beautiful visitor ever seen upon our shores." Displaying a gallantry beyond the call of duty, the jury of professional newsmen refrained from making more than perfunctory remarks about Lola's performance, and, for virtually the first time in her career, she was not assaulted. Apparently the critics thought of her as a celebrated woman who had been at home in the headlines for years, and so did not feel compelled to treat her as a serious actress, dancer, or singer. Americans understood, it seemed, that celebrities didn't have to be talented.

Their praise fired public interest, and *Betley* immediately sold out for the entire run, which was to end on February 1. Willis had scheduled a short engagement, knowing that Lola's talents were limited.

On the basis of her New York success, Willis secured an engagement for her at the Walnut Street Theatre in Philadelphia, and there, in a run of *Betley* that opened on February 10, Lola scored another triumph. It should be noted that the Philadelphia reviewers were even more tight-lipped about Lola's actual performance than their New York colleagues had been, but they were equally lavish in their praise of her beauty. The Philadelphia engagement, which lasted for five weeks, broke box-office records at the Walnut Street Theatre. For the first time in her thirty-three years, Lola had achieved the theatrical stardom for which she had yearned.

While Lola played in Philadelphia, Edward Willis was furiously busy making plans that would capitalize on the public's desire to see her on stage. Taking Lola's own idea, which had run afoul of the British censors, he hired a journeyman dramatist, C. P. T. Ware, to write a play called *Lola Montez in Bavaria.*

Ware read newspaper clippings by the bale, then studied Lola's just-published *Autobiography,* which unfortunately was silent on that period of her life. He finally went to Philadelphia to see the real-life heroine of his drama and spent several days listening to her highly colored reminiscences.

The play that finally took shape was a series of semiconnected sketches, with Lola playing herself in each of them. Their titles tell the story of the play: The Danseuse, The Politician, The Countess, The Revolutionist, The Fugitive. Willis insisted that the principal supporting players be given strong parts, and Lola, wise enough to recognize her own limitations as an actress, allowed some of the other members of the cast to be given the best lines and even the best scenes. In all there were sixteen in the cast, but Lola was the only woman.

The personal appearance tour closed late in March, and Lola returned to New York for rehearsals, which began after she had rested only a few days. During that period she went on a buying spree, purchasing a carriage and a team of horses, two fur coats, and enough clothes to last an ordinary woman a decade.

The opening of *Lola Montez in Bavaria* at the Broadway Theatre on May 18 confronted the New York drama critics with a dilemma unique in their experience. Lola's performance left everything to be desired; by no stretch of even the most charitable imagination could she be judged as a professional actress. On the other hand, since she was portraying herself, she could hardly be attacked on the grounds that her characterization lacked verisimilitude. Most reviewers solved the problem by pretending it did not exist. They praised her beauty, her wardrobe, and her energy, never suggesting that she delivered her lines in a wooden monotone that was occasionally relieved by near-hysterical outbursts. A few of the critics hinted that her performance was less than polished, but Lola was still enjoying a honeymoon with the American press, and none of the critics attacked her.

Reviews meant little to the theatergoing public in any case. The theater was sold out for the four weeks of the engagement, which prompted Willis to extend it for another two weeks. The high point of *Lola Montez in Bavaria* came in the scene called The Revolutionist: Lola came on stage armed with a whip, which she used to defend herself from a mob that tried to assault her. The audience invariably applauded when she came on stage carrying the whip and cheered her when she drove off the mob, player by player.

Her success on stage prompted Lola to start carrying a whip around New York, and she even bought herself a silver-handled lash, which she had initialed with small diamonds. On occasion, the newspapers reported, she cracked the whip when a shop clerk failed to wait on her quickly or when a waiter in a restaurant did not bring her order promptly. She did manage to refrain from carrying the whip when she dined at Pfaff's, the restaurant favored by theater people and authors. Instinct told her that she would be laughed out of the place if she carried her offstage play-acting too far.

The press referred to her as the belle of New York, which was not an accurate representation. Lola could have been the most popular woman in town, had she wished, but she led an exceptionally circumspect private life and was usually seen publicly in the company of Willis, Ware, or some of the supporting players in her play. For the first time in her adult life, she was earning substantial sums of money regularly; she had no need for the money or influence of a wealthy protector. It annoyed her that even in America the ladies of society refused to accept her, but she appeared determined to break down the barriers that separated her from them. "I am a countess," she complained to a reporter from the *Tribune*, "so I don't see why these women who are nothing at all should turn their backs when I come into a room."

The best way to break down prejudice, Lola decided, was to lead an exemplary life. She indulged in no romances, and although many men sought her favors, a watchful press could detect no lovers in her life.

The publication of her *Autobiography*, with its emphasis on the fanciful and the melodramatic, had earned her large royalties while doing nothing to improve Lola's social standing. "The ladies of this city," she told the *Tribune* reporters, "love to read about me, but they are afraid I will contaminate them if we should meet."

Lola's next move exemplified why their behavior, such a mystery to Lola, was inevitable. Money had been a problem for so much of her life that she wanted to earn as much as she could while her popularity lasted, and Lola came up with a new scheme that was profitable, tasteless, and utterly characteristic of her. She rented the ballroom at her hotel, the Howard, and advertised in the newspapers that she would give a series of receptions there. Anyone could be admitted for the price of $1 and in return be rewarded with fifteen minutes of Lola's company. The visitor would be entitled to shake her hand, "stand near" her, and converse with her in English, French, Spanish, German, or Polish.

More than 500 people crowded the hotel's ballroom at the first of these functions, and the second brought out more than 1,000, which made it necessary for the police to summon reserves to control the crowd. Lola survived the experience, but her enthusiastic followers snatched her gloves, veil, and one of her shoes as souvenirs. The drawing rooms of New York society were still locked, presumably forever, and Lola had to console herself with the fat bank account she was accumulating.

Hurt by the snubs of the people she considered her peers, Lola began to cast an eye toward other, greener pastures. A familiar restlessness gripped her. When Willis came to her with a list of cities that were asking for her appearance in *Lola Montez in Bavaria*, she accepted only New Orleans. She had not told him her private reasons, knowing he would try to veto her latest plan.

[CHAPTER XX]

New Orleans greeted Lola Montez with cheers when she opened there in July, 1852. Every seat was sold in advance for her three-week engagement, and Lola captivated the multilingual residents of the city by making a curtain-call speech in English, French, and Spanish. In the final edition of her *Autobiography*, Lola reserved some of her warmest remarks for New Orleans, observing that she had never enjoyed greater hospitality elsewhere.

At the end of her second week there, she sent a telegram to Willis in New York, informing him that she was canceling the rest of her tour and terminating her business relationship with him. He hurried to New Orleans, where Lola explained matters somewhat more fully: her stocks in the Eureka mines were paying handsome dividends, and she wanted to visit the mines herself. Lola had caught the most virulent disease of the age, gold fever.

Willis tried to argue with her, but Lola would not be dissuaded. She saw no reason why she should not make herself independently wealthy for the rest of her life. It took hours of arguing before Willis could persuade her to appear on the stage in San Francisco. Lola was finally convinced that he was giving her sensible advice. A stage appearance would pay her expenses, and she would have an opportunity to hunt for gold, too.

Late in July she sailed across the Gulf of Mexico from New Orleans in a 500-ton steamer, accompanied by two maids, her spaniel, and a few worldly possessions. Most travelers bound for California packed their earthly goods in a small carpet bag; Lola was carrying 39 pieces of luggage.

She disembarked at San Juan del Norte, in Nicaragua, which was the gateway to the gold fields of the American West. Instead of traveling across the breadth of the Central American jungles in the small coach that was available to her, she turned the carriage over to her maids and prepared to make the journey on horseback. So many robbers lurked in the interior that travelers crossed to the Pacific side of Nicaragua in convoys, but Lola seemed ready for any adventure. On the morning of her departure from San Juan del Norte, she appeared in a tailored shirt, breeches, and boots; a broad-brimmed hat covered her hair, and she had a pair of loaded pistols in her belt. She also carried her whip, and on the tedious ride through the jungle she amused her companions by felling leaves on high tree branches with the lash. Her aim was unerring, according to interviews given the San Francisco press by some of her fellow travelers.

The largest steamer on the Pacific run, the *Northerner*, was taking on passengers when Lola reached the coast of Nicaragua. She went on board at once, but was forced to wait in the stifling tropical heat for the better part of a week while other passengers continued to arrive. To pass the time, she went on several excursions into the interior, accompanied by Patrick Purdy Hull, a native of Ohio who was the editor of the San Francisco *Whig*.

A hard-drinking, personable man in his mid-thirties, Hull had lived in California ever since the discovery of gold there in 1848 and, thanks to his profession, knew as much about the gold fields as any man alive. Whatever Lola's reasons for forming the association, Hull was her constant companion by the time the *Northerner* finally sailed, carrying more than 400 passengers, the largest load of mail ever to reach San Francisco up to that time, and Lola Montez' 39 pieces of luggage.

Before the voyage ended, Pat Hull was thoroughly infatuated with Lola and, when not at her side, wrote her impassioned letters, which she carefully preserved. The extent to which she reciprocated his feelings is debatable. There can be no question that she found him charming, but neither in her *Autobiography* nor elsewhere did she ever indicate that she loved him. Before they reached San Francisco, Hull had proposed marriage, and Lola had said no.

The tenor of Hull's letters indicates that Lola also refused to engage in an affair with him. Some of her early biographers claimed that the "moral climate" of America caused a change in her approach to life, a notion that is dubious at best. What is far more likely is that she was still taking great care to do nothing that would offend her American public.

Since the days she had been forced to fend for herself as a streetwalker in Brussels, Lola had not given much evidence that she cared what people thought of her morals or lack of them. Consciously or otherwise, her attitude was more that of a man: although she did not go out of her way to advertise her affairs, neither did she try to conceal them. She lived as she pleased, defying the conventions of Europe.

Now that the Old World had shunned her and she had proved to herself that she could achieve great success in the New World, she exhibited a caution never before noted in her character Since Americans were recognized as the most Puritanical of people, she chose, at this time at least, to live according to their rules. It seems unlikely that she would have rejected Hull's bed had she met him in Europe. Her instincts were those of a chameleon, and her surface colors changed in the United States—for a time—but it is nevertheless reasonable to assume that her own standard remained opportunistic and that conventional morality still meant nothing to her.

After a voyage of fourteen days, Lola landed in San Francisco, where she was accorded a tumultuous welcome. Many accounts of her arrival were published, no two of them alike. The size of the crowd ranges from 1,000 persons, which is probable, to 10,000, which is unlikely. She is greeted by one brass band, that of the Volunteer Fire Brigade, which is reasonable, or by "a dozen bands," which is absurd. Let it suffice that America's toughest, fastest-growing, most wide-open city extended a hearty greeting to a kindred spirit.

Lola and San Francisco seemed made for each other. Courage, flamboyance, and candor were the qualities most admired, and since virtually everyone in town was an adventurer of sorts, no one could point a finger of scorn at a woman who was forced to live by her wits. London had frowned at Lola's exaggerated style and history, Paris tolerated them, and New York tried to ignore them. But San Francisco understood and heartily approved.

A crowd of more than 5,000 men, according to the San Francisco *Herald,* escorted Lola to her hotel, the Russ House, and an even larger throng gathered in the street outside, begging her to come out onto the balcony. Within minutes Lola learned her first lesson about the differences between this frontier metropolis and the older, established cities of the East. San Francisco carried a chip on its shoulder and was inclined to interpret thoughtless or unknowing gestures as deliberate slights. A group of prominent citizens called on Lola immediately after her arrival; she received the gentlemen without delay, intending to ignore the clamor below her windows. The public, she believed, should pay for the privilege of seeing her. Pat Hull and theater owner John Lewis Baker quickly convinced her she was making a mistake. If the people conceived the notion that she thought she was too good for them, she would be mobbed in the streets, any theater in which she appeared would be wrecked, and she would be driven out of town.

Lola accepted the advice and, going out onto her balcony, blew kisses to the crowd. The men below roared their approval. The noise was so great that Lola could not make a speech. She impulsively threw a scarf over her balcony railing—a dangerous gesture, as it turned out. Men stampeded as they tried to gain possession of the favor, and five persons were injured in the crush.

Perhaps the most notable difference between San Francisco and the cities of the eastern seaboard could be seen in the attitude of the ladies of the community toward the newcomer. Judges, high-ranking state officials, and members of the U.S. Congress brought their wives with them when they called, and among those who left their cards were the wives of bank presidents and other prominent citizens. No one in San Francisco, respectable or not, seemed inclined to snub the young woman whose lurid background placed her beyond acceptance elsewhere.

For the second time in her life, Lola had achieved social stature, this time without the aid of a monarch who forced his subjects to go through the motions of paying respect to her. But she quickly learned that there was a different sort of discrimination at work in the raw frontier city. There were only two kinds of women in San Francisco: married ladies, hence respectable; and single women—prostitutes, almost without exception. The *Herald* estimated that the ratio of men to women was fifteen to one; the *Whig* called that figure too conservative. It was inevitable that many men would misinterpret the status of a beautiful woman whose wardrobe had been designed on the principle that her charms were well worth seeing.

The impetuous, the ignorant, and the woman-hungry reacted accordingly, and Lola had her hands full. Men called to her in the streets when she ventured out alone; others lunged at her in public; and one afternoon she returned to her suite to find that two intoxicated giants from the gold fields had broken in and were waiting for her. She managed the situation in her own way by carrying her whip with her whenever she left the hotel, never hesitating to use it when accosted. The two intruders fared worse: Lola sent them flying into the rutted dirt street by firing her pistols above, and not too far above, their heads.

Pat Hull continued to press Lola, daily asking her to marry him, but she procrastinated. The advantages of married life in such a place were obvious, but she had no intention of spending the rest of her days there unless, to be sure, she made a killing in the gold fields. She put Hull off with one excuse after another, claiming she was too busy organizing her life to think in terms of taking a husband.

It is true that she had little free time. She made two brief trips to the gold fields, but it was autumn now, the prospectors were beginning to drift into town for the winter, and she was advised to wait until the following spring before going off into the wilderness to stake a claim of her own. In the meantime her living costs were high, and the time had come to start earning money again.

John L. Baker offered her the starring role in *The School for Scandal,* which he planned to present at his American Theatre, and Lola accepted. Nowhere else in the world could she conceivably have been asked to play the exacting part of Lady Teazle, but San Francisco was indifferent to the finer points of acting. The necklines of Lola's eighteenth-century costumes were daring, she looked gorgeous, and no man asked for more.

Pat Hull reviewed the play for the *Whig* and, not surprisingly, compared Lola to all of the world's great actresses, past and present, none of whom he had ever seen. Other critics were more restrained, one or two even commenting in passing that there were moments when a certain lack of training seemed evident. For the most part, however, they followed the example of their New York colleagues, awarding Lola the praise she had come to expect as her due in the United States.

There were no vacant seats in the house during the three weeks that Lola made her own brand of theatrical history as Lady Teazle. Then, after a short rest, she appeared again under John Baker's management, this time in a series of dances at the Metropolitan Theatre. Again she scored a triumph, the hunger of her audiences for the sight of a lovely woman overcoming any deficiencies in her performance.

San Francisco, it seemed, could not get enough of Lola, and Baker's announcement that he would present a production of *Lola Montez in Bavaria* was greeted with enthusiasm. But this time Lola and the theater owner were too ambitious. The sets were difficult to create, and, more important, there were few actors of stature in the area who were capable of carrying the main burden of the play.

Soon after rehearsals began in early April, 1853, Lola's colleagues learned there was more to her nature than beauty and feminine charm. She lost her temper with the director, quarreled with the actors, and dismissed the scenic designer when he tried to defend himself in a fight with her. Baker attempted to restore order, but Lola was in such an ugly mood by this time that she took her whip to him, chasing him out of his own theater into the street.

The quarrels were patched, but they left their scars, and for many years after the opening in mid-May of 1853, the presentation of *Lola Montez in Bavaria* was regarded as the worst ever to grace San Francisco's boards. Even the most devoted of Lola's admirers were numbed by her wretched performance; it was said that only Pat Hull applauded her when the curtain fell at the end of the first act. By the middle of the second act, there were hisses and catcalls, followed by a shower of pennies descending on the stage.

Lola promptly lost her celebrated temper, halted her performance, and stepped to the footlights, where she cursed her tormentors in several languages. She then resumed the play, but half of her audience had walked out, and those who remained were apathetic. For the first time in America, an audience had accorded her the treatment that had been customary in Europe.

Lola Montez in Bavaria closed after its fifth performance, and Lola postponed her plans to appear in yet another play, *The Maid of Saragossa.* Men were returning to the gold fields, the spring fever of prospectors was mounting, and the theater had temporarily lost its appeal. Pat Hull's proposals of marriage began to seem more attractive, and he may have been surprised when Lola accepted him. The couple were married on July 1, 1853, at the Church of the Mission Dolores, Lola again putting aside the fact that an English court had only granted her first husband a separation. The ceremony was performed in the presence of a distinguished company that included California Governor and Mrs. James E. Wainwright, several judges, and two members of the U.S. Congress.

After a reception given at the Russ House by their friends, more than 300 men availed themselves of the opportunity to kiss the bride. Then Lola and her new husband went off to Sacramento, the capital of the gold country, for their honeymoon. Among those who saw them off were U.S. Senator John B. Wells of California and Mayor George W. Baker of San Francisco.

Sacramento, its population swollen by the annual arrival of thousands of gold hunters, was a strange mixture of the urbane and the primitive. Brick buildings had replaced the wooden shacks that prospectors had thrown up four years earlier, and the Hotel Orleans was one of the most luxurious hostelries in America, its clientele usually paying their bills in gold dust. There were two well-appointed theaters in town, and expensive restaurants served meals that could rival those prepared in New York's most elegant establishments. It was true that no sidewalks had been built as yet, that most disputes were still settled by an exchange of gunfire, and that there were few women in the town other than the inmates of a long row of cabins, which, the *Democratic State Journal* declared, were the shame of the community.

Pat Hull, who was far from wealthy, quickly learned that his bride had no intention of changing her living standards by trying to eke out an existence on his small income. Having engaged lodgings at a boardinghouse, he was mortified when Lola stamped out after taking one look at the quarters. Reserving the best suite at the Orleans, she appeared in the dining room wearing some of her most dazzling jewels, none of which Hull had given her.

The marriage was doomed from the outset. Lola again demonstrated how much less successful she was in selecting husbands than in selecting lovers. She took so much camping equipment with her on trips up the Sacramento, Feather, and American Rivers that the embarrassed Hull later said he "worked harder than the damned pack horses." The men panning for gold in the Sierra Nevada Mountains were unaware of Lola's identity and would not have cared, had they known. Many of them had not seen a woman in months, the newcomer was attractive and naturally flirtatious, and they tried to act accordingly.

Lola protested in vain to her new husband that she could take care of herself, that no man could approach her when she was armed with her whip and a brace of pistols. Hull, insisting that his own manhood would be questioned if he failed to protect her, tried to call a halt to their expedition. His wife refused to listen.

By the time they returned to Sacramento after spending six weeks in the wilderness, Lola was suntanned and strong; Hull was exhausted. He had also been drinking too much, and he was anxious to return to his work on the *Whig*. At this unfortunate moment Lola was offered a theatrical engagement in Sacramento. She accepted it, informing her husband that she earned more in a single performance than he could make in a month. Hull went off to San Francisco without her, and there were those who said the marriage was ended. Lola, who surely would have agreed, kept her own counsel.

[CHAPTER XXI]

Lola, having gone to the California gold fields to find a fortune, was faring better in the more familiar surroundings of the theater. She performed as a dancer for her Sacramento audiences, and, as word of her glamour and beauty spread, men traveled hundreds of miles through the wilderness to see and applaud her. Never before had she known such a devoted following—what did it matter that the few members of her audiences who knew anything about the dance shuddered and sometimes demanded that the management return their money? Most of the men who roared their approval at her Saturday night performances thought she was magnificent, and the *State Journal*, its editorial tongue firmly in cheek, called her "Our very own Countess, the Queen of the Gold Country."

Marriage, Lola found, was a protection to her in the company of lonely frontier dwellers, and she made an effort to improve her shaky relationship with Pat Hull. Comfortable steamers made regular overnight runs on the Sacramento River between San Francisco and Sacramento; soon the Hulls were reunited and spending part of every week in each of the cities. On Friday nights they traveled to Sacramento, where Lola spent the day rehearsing for her evening performance, and on Sunday nights they returned to San Francisco so Hull could attend to his duties on the *Whig*.

This arrangement made it easier for Lola to handle her admirers, but her love of luxury did little to improve the marriage.

Her hotel suites in both San Francisco and Sacramento were far beyond the pocketbook of Pat Hull, who could not afford to dine nightly in expensive restaurants, pay the wages of his wife's maids, or indulge her near-mania for clothes. Hull was paying the price of marriage to a celebrated woman who lacked any desire to settle down into middle-class domesticity, and he continued to take refuge in the bottle.

A visit to the Eureka mine, which was still paying large dividends, gave Lola a new ambition late in 1853. Hull accompanied her on the journey and apparently managed to persuade her that their marriage could be salvaged if they would begin a new life together. He would sell his interest in the *Whig*, he told her, and buy her a home in the gold country, if she in return would give up her theatrical career. The idea appealed to Lola, perhaps because the experience would be new to her. On the return to Sacramento from the Eureka mines, she found a community she wanted to live in. It was a little town, Grass Valley, which stood on the edge of a plain in the foothills of the Sierras.

Thick pines stretched out toward the horizon in every direction, and fish and game were plentiful—all of which made it unnecessary for people to have steady employment in order to obtain shelter, fuel, and food. There were other advantages that drew newcomers to the place. Grass Valley was remarkably peaceful for a frontier town, probably because of the unusually large number of women and children there. Married prospectors whose wives had joined them gravitated toward the community because it offered stability, and out of a total population of approximately 1,500, more than 300 residents were married women. For their protection the town boasted a sheriff and two deputies.

There was yet another attraction that may have been the decisive one in Lola's mind. Grass Valley was located in the heart of the gold country. Everyone in town, women and children included, searched the area for the precious metal, establishing claims to parcels of land.

Lola and Hull returned to San Francisco long enough for the editor to sell his interest in the *Whig* and his real estate and for

Lola to inform the press of their decision to retire to the little town in the foothills of the Sierra Nevadas. Pat Hull's former partners later said he seemed happier than he had been at any time since his marriage. He would be supporting his wife now, and life would be reordered.

The couple rented a house on the edge of town, the largest in the area. Lola shipped all of her belongings there, including some expensive furniture she had purchased in San Francisco. Two servants, a cook, and a ladies' maid followed her to the wilderness, ensuring that the rustic life would not be spoiled for her by the necessity of cooking or engaging in household chores.

Hull and Lola arrived in Grass Valley in December, 1853, almost six months after their marriage, and celebrated Christmas in their log house. The retired editor loved hunting, and the retired actress-adventuress soon acquired a taste for the sport. They made numerous trips together into the forests and mountains—Pat Hull's recipe for a happy marriage appeared to be successful.

The citizens of Grass Valley had been amazed to learn that the famous Lola Montez would be their neighbor; new surprises soon awaited the housewives of the town. They had anticipated Lola's arrival with some nervousness, assuming she would patronize them. They soon discovered, however, that she put on no airs, treated everyone as her equal, and did not hesitate to do her share of the work when everyone in the area went to the local hall for potluck suppers.

What they did not realize, of course, was that Lola was still acting. Always the chameleon, she was still changing her coloration to fit the circumstances in which she found herself. Offstage, she had always been a superior actress—it was not difficult for her to make the transition to a simple life in a tiny town located in the California wilderness. Much more difficult had been her roles as a child in Scotland, as the bride of an officer in India, not to mention her biggest starring part as the power behind the throne of Bavaria.

She chatted with her neighbors about various high points in her life story, unfailingly sacrificing truth to drama. She proved herself ingenious in devising games for the children of the community. And she endeared herself to Grass Valley wives by behaving with demure circumspection in the presence of their husbands and the bachelors of the area. No one who met her in the California wilderness would have guessed she had spent the better part of her adult life as a courtesan.

In the spring of 1854, a miner gave Lola a bear cub he had captured; she tamed the animal, named it Major, and took it with her everywhere. Hull, who regarded bears as treacherous beasts, tried in vain to persuade Lola to part with her pet. As Major grew to his full size of more than 300 pounds, his attachment to Lola became so great that he would permit no man to approach her when he was nearby. Major made no exception of Lola's husband, which neither helped Hull's opinion of him nor improved marital relations.

Other more serious stresses were weakening the fabric of the marriage. For the first time since the days of Lola's adolescent experience as a housewife in India, she had virtually nothing to occupy her time. She enjoyed her hunting trips with Hull, but they kept her busy only one or two days each week. Fishing bored her, she had little or nothing in common with the other women of Grass Valley, and her servants took care of all domestic chores.

The problem was complicated by her husband's inability to develop new interests. Hull, too, had worked for a living ever since he had been a boy. It was difficult for him to relax, and he found time hanging heavily on his hands. He spoke of a newspaper he intended to publish for the people of the mining country, but printing equipment was expensive and difficult to obtain, and his plans did not progress beyond the talking stage.

It must have annoyed him when Lola began to spend an hour or two at her desk every day, writing and embellishing a new version of her *Autobiography*. New York and Boston publishers had offered her substantial sums for the book if she would include more material on her American experiences; busy obliging them, she would permit no interruption when she retired to her private sitting room.

Her work as an author soon led to a return to the theater. Her activities in the United States had been limited, she claimed; she needed more raw material from which to fashion the new chapters. A return to the stage would meet this need, and she was, fortuitously, swamped with offers. Word had spread through the mining camps of California and Nevada that she was living in the area; many of these towns had built primitive theaters, and their residents, overwhelmingly male, were starved for entertainment. Money meant little to the miners, who spent their gold as rapidly as they acquired it, and Lola was offered as much for a single night's appearance as she had earned for a full week in New York or Philadelphia.

She insisted that the theater, as such, no longer meant anything to her, but Hull found it difficult to accept her assertion that she merely wanted to acquire additional material for her book. He refused to give his consent. Lola, of course, had never been one to seek someone else's approval before doing what she wanted, and she did not begin now.

She accepted a number of engagements, leaving Hull with the unappealing alternatives of sulking at home or accompanying her and sulking backstage while miners shouted to his wife to show more of her legs when she danced. It was almost inevitable that he would drink heavily again and that Lola would treat him with increasing indifference and contempt.

At this critical point in her marriage to Hull, probably in the spring of 1854, Lola met a man known to posterity only as Adler. A German by birth, he had come to America a few years earlier; according to some accounts he was a baron who had dropped his title, while others characterized him as a doctor. A broad-shouldered giant who could be a gentleman one moment and a bully the next, he was amply supplied with funds, did not bother to search for gold, and spent most of his time hunting and fishing.

Lola met him when she went off alone on one of her trips to perform in a mining town. Adler, not at all discouraged by the fact that she was married, began to pay court to her. Lola found him fascinating, in part because his manners recalled those of the polished Europeans she had known previously, and partly because of his encyclopedic knowledge of the New World wilderness. He could tell her the name of every tree and flower, every bird they saw fly overhead, every animal in the forest or fish in the streams.

Knowledge had always impressed Lola, and the most important men in her life—Liszt, Dujarier, and Ludwig—had been intellectuals. While it might be going too far to say that she fell in love with Adler, she was infatuated, and, at some time in the summer or early autumn of 1854, she went off on an extended trip into the mountains with him.

Whether this journey took place before or after she and Pat Hull separated is a point that has never been clarified. Some of Lola's early, loyal biographers insisted that Hull had already deserted her, while others, writing somewhat later and perhaps trying to add fresh sensationalism to her story, said it was the affair with Adler that caused the final disruption of her marriage. In the second and third versions of her *Autobiography*, Lola treated the subject with a delicacy that verged on coyness. She described Adler as a handsome near-genius to whom women were drawn, a "friend" who had been helpful in teaching her wilderness lore.

In any event, Pat Hull returned to San Francisco, where friends helped him in his battle against liquor. He eventually went back to work as editor of the *Whig*, this time as an employee rather than a part owner. He lived only four years longer, during which time he neither wrote about Lola nor discussed her with his friends. He not only refused to answer questions about their married life, he refused even to mention Lola's name, thereby thwarting the curiosity of his contemporaries and contributing nothing to posterity.

Meanwhile Lola was enjoying a rare period of contentment. Her home in the wilderness, the adulation of the miners—not to mention the wages they paid for an occasional stage appearance—and her affair with Adler combined to give her a kind of life style that was, for the moment, very much to her satisfaction. A correspondent for the San Francisco *Herald* visited her on December 13, 1854, at her log house in Grass Valley, and wrote about her with wonder:

> Lola Montez is living a quiet and apparently cozy life. Her companion is her tame brown bear, Major, who spends his days in the house with her, and is retired at night to his own shack outside her wind w. She is also surrounded by her pet birds and dogs, and her mare is always available in the stables at the rear of the house. There are other creatures on her property, too—turkeys, chickens, sheep, goats and pigs.
>
> The bear remains at home when she rides off on her mountain rambles, and on these occasions her companion is the mare, who responds at once to her touch, but will allow no one else near.
>
> Surely it is a strange metamorphosis to find the woman who has gained a world-wide notoriety, and has played a part upon the stage of life with powerful potentates, and with whose name Europe and the world are familiar, finally settled down at home in the mountain wilds of California.

Adler paid his last visit to Lola's Grass Valley house early in 1855, and although he continued to live in the mountains, she did not meet him again. Her neighbors were unable to discover whether they had parted by mutual consent or whether Lola had dismissed him. It did not cross their minds—perhaps because she was unperturbed by his disappearance—that Adler might have tired of her.

By early spring Lola was restless again. She had completed the new version of her *Autobiography*, which she had mailed to a New York publisher, and the peace of the wilderness was beginning to pall. With the peripatetic quality in her nature demanding fresh excitement, she decided to return to San Francisco and plan her future. She was now thirty-seven years old and anxious to better her financial standing before her glamour faded.

It was not easy, Lola discovered, to pull up stakes overnight. Having purchased her house in the summer of 1854, she now let it be known that she was willing to sell. The offers she received did not satisfy her, and she waited until she found the right buyer.

The delay proved worth her while; she proudly told an interviewer she had made a profit of $2,000 in gold dust on the deal.

She sold her menagerie, but disposing of Major and the mare presented something of a problem. Determined to turn her horse over to someone who would treat the animal with consideration, she finally settled on a woman who lived nearby. Few people were interested in acquiring a pet bear, and she was afraid Major had lived too long in domesticity to survive in the wilderness. Remembering a miner who had expressed a fondness for the beast, she went off to see him, finding him after a two-day ride into the mountains. He accompanied her to Grass Valley, and Lola was so happy to find the right master for Major that she allowed sentiment to take precedence over business. She made the man a gift of the bear, one of the few times in her life that she showed such open-handed generosity.

Lola finally left for San Francisco in May of 1855. Having sold most of her furniture to the buyers of her house, she was encumbered only by her personal possessions and wardrobe, which had grown smaller during her wilderness sojourn. She was accompanied by a single cart carrying twenty-three pieces of luggage.

Opening the mail that awaited her in San Francisco, she decided she must have been guided by fate when she decided to leave Grass Valley. Among the letters was an offer she found irresistible, and, in accepting it, Lola was launched on what would prove to be the last of her real adventures.

[CHAPTER XXII]

Australia in the mid-nineteenth century was a land of contradictions. A frontier continent as crude in many ways as the northern California Lola was leaving, it was nevertheless overlaid with a patina of the English civilization that had rejected her. Originally settled by convicts sent there from the British Isles in 1787, the colony had grown slowly, attracting adventurers and men who wanted to raise cattle or establish sheep farms. Gold had been discovered in 1851, and Australia was now enjoying a population explosion and economic boom similar to that in the California Lola Montez now called her home.

The men of Australia were so starved for entertainment that they were willing to pay any price for it, and the offer made to Lola was the best of her theatrical career. A San Francisco admirer was responsible, Lola discovered, one who, of all the men in her life, had a background most nearly resembling her own. Noel Follin, nearly fifteen years younger than Lola, had already lived an amazingly full life. The son of a former brothel keeper, Follin had run through an inheritance left him by his first wife and then earned his living by holding scores of different jobs. Married while still in his teens, he had left a wife and two children in the Midwest when he came to San Francisco.

There he had drifted into the theater, where his handsome face won him several small parts, but he was no actor and aspired to be a theater owner and producer. He had worked as a ticket seller in a San Francisco theater when Lola played there, and in her he had seen the key to his near future. Not bothering to obtain her consent or even tell her what he was doing, he wrote to the theater owners of Australia, representing himself as her personal manager and indicating that she would be willing to come to that country for a price.

The theatrical entrepreneurs of Australia made their bids, which Follin promptly rejected, and a long period of dickering began. The theater owners kept raising their offers until finally they went over Follin's head and appealed direct to Lola. It was this letter that awaited her in San Francisco.

Knowing nothing of the matter, Lola went to Follin, whose name was mentioned in the letter. He confessed what he had done and showed her his correspondence, explaining that he had intended to approach her once he felt the offers were high enough. Lola, both impressed and amused, instructed him to accept the juicy offer just made and then hired him as her manager, at $100 a week.

Together Lola and Follin hired actors and actresses for their company, no talent worthy of the name being available in Australia. In all they engaged six supporting players, four of them men; both the women were middle-aged, and neither had ever been renowned for her beauty. Early in June they sailed from San Francisco on board the clipper *Frances*, which was bound for Sydney by way of Honolulu, the principal city of the Sandwich Islands.

Lola's attitude toward her fellow players was professional enough, and she rehearsed with them every morning and afternoon. But she spent her free hours on the voyage alone, locking herself into her first-class cabin with a spaniel, her one remaining pet. There were no men among her fellow passengers who interested her, and the other actors lost money when they bet that Follin would become her lover within a few days. When the *Frances* put into Honolulu, Lola remained on board during the three days that livestock, fresh fruit, and casks of water were loaded on the decks. Follin spent the time ashore, taking the dog with him, but Lola stayed in her cabin during daylight hours, wandering onto the deck only after dark when she could not be seen from the wharves. Her fellow passengers, including her own associates, thought her behavior eccentric but dismissed it.

In mid-August, after a voyage that lasted more than two months, the *Frances* finally sailed into Jackson Harbor, Sydney, which was crowded with more than 400 vessels of every description. The great gold rush was still at its height, and Lola plunged into a madhouse. The suite she had engaged was not available, and Follin had to restrain her when she threatened to sail for home. Only with difficulty could she be persuaded to accept other quarters.

Sydney was the oldest city in Australia—or New South Wales, as the country was called—but living there was primitive even by the standards of someone who had buried herself in the California wilderness. The hotels were new and inadequately furnished; service was slipshod; meals were atrocious. The menus were the same everywhere, even in the so-called first-class restaurants. The usual first course was a thick soup of tripe and sharp, locally grown vegetables. The main course was a cold roast of either beef or mutton, served with a whole loaf of heavy bread. Patrons, expected to slice what they wanted off the bread, were charged accordingly. There were no salads, vegetables, or fruits available, and desserts were more or less nonexistent. Since the same meals were servd at noon and in the evening, Lola soon became heartily sick of the fare.

What bothered her more than the inconveniences was the attitude Sydney displayed toward her. Certainly she was as well known in this city as she was in Europe or the United States, but New South Wales had other things on its mind. Gold was the principal preoccupation, and men devoted what spare time they had to the forging of the country's constitution.

To make matters still worse, Sydney had just adopted a sweetheart. Catherine Hayes, an Irish singer known as "the sweet swan," had begun an engagement there a fortnight earlier and had achieved such a resounding success that the newspapers were proposing, in all seriousness, that she be granted honorary Australian citizenship. The arrival of Lola Montez created no more than a mild stir.

She opened at the Victoria Theatre on August 26 in a truncated version of *Lola Montez in Bavaria.* She played to a full house and achieved a modest success, but the most enthusiastic applause of the evening was reserved for her leading man, a Mr. Lambert, who played the part of King Ludwig. At the end of the performance, Lola graciously presented Lambert with a box of cigarettes, having recently become an addict herself. The next day she was furious when the newspapers devoted the bulk of their praise to Lambert.

So few patrons bought tickets that Lola changed her repertory after three performances, substituting a new play, *Yelva, or the Orphan of Russia,* which she had allegedly written herself. It may be that Noel Follin, who had ambitions as a playwright, was the real author. In any event, nothing is known of the play; no copies of the script have survived, and it was never played anywhere except Sydney, where it expired after three dismal performances.

Lola was growing desperate, and as a last resort she introduced her dance recital, which had drawn cheers in the mining towns of California and Nevada. The high point of the evening was her "Spider Dance," which the San Francisco *Herald* had hailed as a "delight of terpsichore." Wearing a low-cut, calf-length gown of black silk, she danced as if covered with spiders. Writhing, wriggling, and hurling herself about the stage with reckless abandon, Lola rid herself of the imaginary spiders, one by one, stamping on them in pseudo-Spanish style as they fell to the floor.

California had considered the dance naughty and had loved it. But New South Wales, although a frontier land in many respects, was conscious of its English heritage and had cultivated a Victorian veneer. Men might visit the brothels of the Jackson Harbor waterfront in private, but in public they were as respectable as any solid Londoner. Lola's dance drew a stony, outraged silence, and that only because the almost exclusively male audience remembered its manners and refrained from hissing.

Lola took the lack of enthusiasm as a personal insult, and the final version of her *Autobiography* shows how little she appreciated or understood the Australian mentality. Certainly she had been spurned, and it may be that in her loneliness she turned to Noel Follin. It is generally believed that their affair began at this time—at least, the other members of the company were convinced that they were now intimate.

Lola made up her mind to cut short her Sydney engagement, a decision with which the management of the Victoria Theatre heartily agreed. The tour was paying its expenses, but there were no profits, and Lola made an attempt to cut back her cast by discharging one of the actresses, a Mrs. Feddes or Fiddes. The older woman protested, even though Lola offered to pay her fare and expenses back to San Francisco. They had words, Follin naturally supported Lola, and Mrs. Feddes was discharged.

Mrs. Feddes went to the Sydney court flourishing her contract and was granted a writ of attachment ordering Lola to pay her wages in full or lose her scenery and costumes. A local bailiff named Brown was given the task of serving the writ, and on the evening of September 6, when Lola was scheduled to sail for Melbourne, he boarded the coastal steamer to hand her the paper.

One of the ship's officers told Follin that Brown was waiting to serve the writ, and Lola sneaked onto the vessel by way of the steerage. By the time Brown learned of her arrival, she had locked herself in her cabin. The intrepid Brown asked that a message be taken to Lola: he intended to remain on board until he could serve the writ. If necessary he would sail all the way to Melbourne.

Lola sent a message in reply. She was ready to accept the writ but thought it only fair to warn him that she had removed all of her clothes.

The thought of serving the document to a naked woman was too much for the bailiff, who gave up the attempt. The captain of the steamer put him ashore at the Heads, about twenty miles from the city, and he returned to Sydney to tell the story on himself. The citizens of New South Wales were vastly amused, to be sure, but the incident confirmed their low opinion of Lola Montez, and the proprietors of the two leading theaters, the Victoria and the Prince of Wales, promised that under no circumstances would they book her for another engagement.

Melbourne was the "San Francisco of Australia," the capital of the gold rush, and the setting there was reminiscent of California. In four years the population had soared in the overall Port Philip district from 75,000 to more than a third of a million, and newcomers from every civilized nation on earth were arriving daily. Entire cities sprang up overnight, prices were exorbitant, and most of the amenities of life were lacking.

Melbourne was suffering from such an intense gold fever that Lola's arrival went almost unnoticed. There were no sheets on her bed, despite the fact that she paid more for her suite than her rooms in New York. The food, she immediately decided, was inedible, and the fare in the city's restaurants was even worse than the meals her hotel served. She comforted herself with the thought that in a city of gold miners she would repeat her California triumphs.

Again she misread the Australian temperament. The local correspondent of the London *Era* filed an unsettling review:

Lola Montez made her debut in Melbourne on 21st September, in a short drama allusive to her own Bavarian transactions, but the piece was lacking in taste or dramatic subtlety, and might well have borne curtailment. There was a very crowded but apathetic audience.

The *ci-devant* Countess of Landsberg seemed determined to preserve her notoriety intact by the selection, but entrenched so far upon decorum in the "Spider Dance" on a subsequent evening that she did not raise the clamor raised in consequence until the objectionable portions were agreed to be omitted.

She is certainly a very singular character, but there is an ever lively and brusque style in her action that seems to catch general approbation. Had she shown a greater sense of dignity and decorum, Melbourne might have taken her to its heart.

The *Era* reporter did not tell the whole story. Lola was hissed when she appeared in *Lola Montez in Bavaria,* and when she did her "Spider Dance," a near-riot ensued, the audience standing on chairs and jeering until it became impossible for her to continue. Ready to walk out of the theater, she realized she would not be paid and continued despite the difficulties, giving an abbreviated performance.

Happy to put Melbourne behind her, Lola went on to an even more boisterous mining city, Geelong. There she suffered the worst embarrassment of her career. On her opening night the audience unleashed a violent barrage of catcalls when she tried to do her dance, and the management had to ring down the curtain. Further humiliation followed when a delegation of prominent citizens headed by a Dr. Milman called on the mayor of Geelong and demanded, "in the name of an outraged community, that a warrant be issued against all repetition of the performances of Mme. Lola Montez at the Theatre Royal."

The mayor and his aldermen went into their council chamber to consider the question, and then rendered their verdict. The law would not sustain them in issuing a warrant unless Dr. Milman and his associates submitted written, sworn statements to the effect that they had seen Lola's performance and had found it offensive. This the members of the self-appointed committee agreed to do.

The matter ended there, however, for the simple reason that Lola, who was at last learning something from her Australian experiences, decided not to fight. Proclaiming that nothing would persuade her to make another appearance on a Geelong stage, she made plans to leave the city immediately. She did not actually go, however, until the proprietor-manager of the Theatre Royal paid her the minimum agreed for a one-week engagement. He lost money on the transaction, but he got rid of her.

By this time it should have been apparent to Lola that she

could not succeed in Australia, but she prepared for a final effort. Before leaving Geelong, she informed the local newspaper, the *Telegraph,* that she and Noel Follin had been married that day, and the account was duly printed. Inasmuch as she already had two living husbands from whom she had not been divorced, this was carrying her bigamy a trifle far. Follin, of course, had a wife and children in the United States.

Follin later denied the story, defying anyone to produce proof that he and Lola had actually been married. He informed the San Francisco press that he agreed to pose as her husband strictly for publicity purposes so that the Victorian citizens of Australia might regard her as a moral woman. A thorough search of the records, made several years later by the editors of the *Telegraph,* substantiated Follin's claim.

Lola nonetheless referred to Follin thereafter as the last of her husbands, even though they parted company before his return to the United States. It is significant that she made no attempt to counter Follin's denial of marriage during the final years of her life. Most of her biographers have agreed with the Australian press, assuming the marriage to be yet another figment of her ever-lively imagination.

In any event, Follin and the other members of the company wanted to leave Australia as soon as possible, but Lola refused to surrender until she scored one triumph. Paying no heed to the advice of the few friends she had made there, she directed Follin to obtain her a booking in the most wide-open town on the continent, the "wicked city" of Ballarat, located in the center of the gold fields.

The necessary arrangements were made, but before Lola and her associates could travel to Ballarat on horseback, the editor of the local newspaper devoted a full-page editorial in his journal, the *Times,* to her forthcoming visit. She was a woman of such low character, he declared, that she should not be allowed to set foot in the community, much less perform there. Ballarat was a growing, thriving city that was trying to live down its reputation of recent years; the depraved Lola Montez was such a corrupting influence that decency would suffer a terrible blow if she acted on its stage.

Lola, shown the editorial when she arrived at the one respectable hotel in the city, the United States House, lost her frayed temper. It would be her great pleasure, she announced, to horsewhip Mr. Robert Seekamp at the first opportunity.

News of her threat was taken to Seekamp, who promptly armed himself with a whip of his own, went to the bar of the hotel, ordered a drink, and waited for trouble to develop.

Follin, informed of Seekamp's presence, refrained from saying anything to Lola. One of the other members of the company inadvertently let the news slip, and Lola went off to her own room, where she changed into a shirt, breeches, and boots. She then hurried down to the bar, brandishing her whip.

"Is there a man named Seekamp here?"

The editor downed his drink and faced her. "I am Robert Seekamp."

"Well, I am Lola Montez," she replied, and lashed at him with her whip.

Seekamp immediately raised his own whip. The horrified witnesses removed themselves from the immediate vicinity and watched the spectacular duel from the safety of the adjoining lobby.

Lola and Seekamp slashed at each other repeatedly, both inflicting considerable damage, neither giving way. It seemed inevitable that one or the other would suffer severe injury before the fight ended, but a group of gold miners who were en route to the bar managed to intervene. These burly men threw themselves at the antagonists, wrenching the whips from them and thus ending the duel.

Seekamp was fortunate to escape with his life. The miners were prepared to lynch him for fighting with a woman, and apparently only the arrival of the constabulary saved him from that fate.

That night Lola Montez appeared on the stage of the only theater in Ballarat to perform her "Spider Dance" before a crowded house. No amount of makeup could conceal the two puffy red streaks on her face or the even uglier marks that covered her arms and chest. The sympathetic miners greeted her with riotous applause, and her dance was cheered from beginning to end.

At the end of her performance, after several curtain calls, she made a brief speech that was quoted by the press around the world. After expressing platitudinous thanks, she unleashed a verbal assault on Seekamp and challenged him again, this time with pistols. The men of Ballarat regarded her as a heroine, and her Australian tour ended on that small note of triumph.

[CHAPTER XXIII]

Lola returned briefly to Sydney, where she was ignored by the theater owners, the press, and the public at large. By now she had had more than enough of frontier living, and wanted a taste of the comforts and refinements she had known in Europe. She and her associates parted company, Follin and the others returning to San Francisco by way of Fiji while Lola took passage for Singapore on the first leg of her homeward journey.

She left Australia on February 17, and although it is known that she subsequently put into Bombay and Calcutta, no details of that portion of her journey have survived. Her first, and only legal, husband was still stationed there, and she presumably went out of her way to avoid him. Several months later she revealed that she had enjoyed brief visits with "old friends" in India but did not disclose their identity.

Around the beginning of May, 1856, Lola reappeared in Paris. Why she elected to pay another visit to a city that had all but disowned her is a mystery that led several of her early biographers to conclude that she had seen Ludwig at his Riviera villa in the mountains outside Nice. There is no proof of such a meeting. Lola's correspondence with Ludwig, found in the rubble of Munich's World War II bombings, offers no clue; if Lola wrote to Ludwig in 1856, that correspondence was removed before the packet of letters was buried in a cornerstone.

Upon arriving in Paris she ordered an expensive new wardrobe from the salon of Worth, the dressmaker who had become fashionable because of the Empress Eugénie's patronage. The elder Dumas, Théophile Gautier, and other leaders of the Paris literary and theatrical worlds whom Lola had known when she lived with Dujarier studiously ignored her presence in their midst. One evening she entered a restaurant just as Gautier was leaving; he looked past her without making a sign of recognition.

There is no satisfactory explanation for such snubs on the part of Lola's old associates. Dumas and many of the others were indifferent to gossip and continued to live as they pleased, setting their own standards. It may be, however, that Lola's notoriety was too great for even the most liberal to tolerate. She had so far exceeded the bounds of good taste that the sensation-mongering Paris press generally referred to her as a "tigress" or a "savage."

But Lola had necessarily developed a thick skin, and in August, when the court of Napoleon III went to Biarritz, she took up residency at nearby St. Jean de Luz. She was seen at watering places and restaurants, sometimes making an appearance at Biarritz, her escorts unnamed by those newspapers that commented on her activities.

Then, early in September, she burst into print again when she wrote an astonishing letter to the newspaper owned by Dujarier's former partner, Girardin, now the most prominent publisher in France. Girardin, who had good cause to remember her, ordered the letter printed in its entirety:

Hotel du Cygne,
St. Jean de Luz,
2nd September, 1856

Gentlemen:

The Belgian newspapers and some printed in this country have asserted that the distinguished French actor, Mauclerc, who, it is reported, has thrown himself from the summits of the Pic du Midi, was caused by domestic troubles for which I was responsible. This is a calumny which M. Mauclerc himself will doubtless be ready to refute. To the best of my knowledge he is still alive and has not done away with himself.

We separated amicably, it is true, after eight days of married life, but urged only by our common and imperious need of personal liberty. It is probable that the tragedy of the Pic du Midi exists only in the imagination of some journalist searching for sensational news.

Trusting to your sense of fairness to insert this explanation in your excellent journal, I remain,

Yours, etc.,
LOLA MONTEZ

The letter, published in *La Presse* on September 5, was the talk of Paris. No one acquainted with Mauclerc, one of the foremost actors in France, had read or heard of the alleged report that he had tried, successfully or unsuccessfully, to commit suicide. Nor had anyone heard even a whisper to the effect that he and Lola had been married but had separated after eight days. Everyone who knew the actor also knew that he had been married for ten years and lived, presumably happily, with his wife and two children.

Mauclerc was enjoying a holiday in Bayonne, and friends made it their urgent business to take a copy of *La Presse* to him. His initial reaction is not known, but his reply indicates that he had a sense of humor:

Bayonne, 9th September, 1856

Sir:

I have read in your issue of the 5th inst. a letter from Lola Montez, wherein there is talk of a suicide of which I have been the victim, and a marriage in which I have been the principal actor.

I am a complete stranger to both of these catastrophes.

I have never had the least intention of throwing myself from the Pic du Midi or from any other peak.

And I do not recollect having had the advantage of marrying—even for eight days—the celebrated Countess of Landsberg. I have not found it necessary to consult with my wife in this matter, as I feel certain she would be reluctant to approve of such a union.

Yours, etc.,
MAUCLERC

The exchange was reprinted in many countries, and Lola enjoyed several days in the headlines. *La Presse* kept the story alive by assigning several reporters the task of finding the records of the church where the alleged marriage had taken place, no civil ceremonies being permitted in France at the time. No evidence was unearthed.

Mauclerc was still amused when a representative of *La Presse* visited him at his Bayonne retreat, but he refused to be quoted again for publication, saying he had nothing to add to his initial letter. His understandably indignant wife was less reticent. Her husband, Mme. Mauclerc declared, was not acquainted with Lola Montez and, to the best of their joint knowledge, had never even met her. A laughing Mauclerc confirmed his wife's statement.

Reporters besieged Lola, who made herself unavailable to the press, sending word from her hotel suite in St. Jean de Luz that the incident was closed. The reporters persisted, surrounding her when she appeared in the lobby of her hotel en route to dinner. Lola promptly lost her temper, threatening to horsewhip any man who continued to annoy her.

The members of the press departed, never doubting that she was in earnest. Thus the strange episode came to a close.

Lola's original letter can hardly be explained on logical grounds. In theory, Lola might have known Mauclerc without his wife's knowledge and elected to embarrass him after he jilted her. But this explanation suffers from an examination of Mauclerc's activities following Lola's return to France in the spring. He was on tour during the entire period, first in Rouen and Lille, then in Lyons. It would have been physically impossible for him to have held any meetings with Lola, who was in Paris.

Apparently, then, Lola was the victim of her own overactive imagination and wrote the letter at a time when she was either desperate for publicity or, possibly, deranged.

Whatever may have prompted her decidedly peculiar act, it cut her off completely from everyone, including her new friends and acquaintances. She was seen for another week in St. Jean, dining alone and taking solitary walks, always dressed beautifully and still exceptionally attractive, but speaking to no one. She then vanished; no one in Paris knew where she had gone, and apparently no one cared.

Three weeks later, at the end of September, she landed in New York on a steamer she had boarded at Brest sixteen days earlier. Only a few reporters were on hand, and she would not discuss the Mauclerc incident with them. When they asked her whether she had married Noel Follin in Australia, she merely smiled and replied, "I prefer to look toward the future, not the past."

If Lola thought that New York would welcome her, she was mistaken. Americans forgave eccentricities far more readily than did the people of most countries, but Lola had gone too far too often. Ladies shunned her and few men wanted to be seen in her company, even though she was still lovely and looked far younger than her thirty-eight years.

Virtually no one visited her suite in the Howard Hotel, where she lived in solitary splendor, her way of life indicating that although she had no friends, she did not lack funds. Theater owners and managers were slow to respond to her suggestion that she appear for them in a new play, and several indicated their belief that the public had grown tired of her.

Autumn and early winter of 1856 were dreary, but Lola had known too much adversity to let her mounting discouragement show. When she dined at Pfaff's, Sherry's, Delmonico's, and other fashionable restaurants—always alone—she appeared in stunning new clothes that set off her still supple figure. She kept in trim by cantering for an hour every morning on a rented horse. She also regularly attended theatrical openings, hoping to call herself to the attention of producers and theater owners.

Even those who most disliked Lola were forced to admire her style, and in early January of 1857 an impresario named J. Bailey Martin came to her with an offer. Martin, who had been associated with P. T. Barnum for a time, was an inveterate gambler. As such he was willing to present Lola in several plays for a one-week run in Albany; if audiences there liked her, he would bring her to New York City in whatever play drew the most enthusiastic response.

Lola agreed and immediately went into rehearsals with a cast that Martin chose with care. All of the other women hired were in their forties and fifties, and none were attractive. On February 2, 1857, Lola opened her engagement at Albany's Green Street Theatre in *The Eton Boy*, which was followed by *The Follies of a Night* and *Lola Montez in Bavaria.*

All three of these slight dramatic efforts were successful, and Lola proved to Martin's satisfaction as well as her own that audiences would still pay to see her, no matter how great her notoriety. Martin kept his word, and made preparations for her return to Broadway.

Lola, apparently nervous about her return to the New York stage, arranged a publicity stunt that would recall her to the attention of New Yorkers. She hired a small skiff and announced that she would cross the Hudson River in it alone, supposedly to win a bet of $1,000. Although she had never sailed a boat, she calmly proposed to make a crossing through ice floes from the Palisades of New Jersey to a point near the Battery.

On the appointed day a handsomely attired Lola, who had spent the previous night in New Jersey, made her appearance during a violent blizzard. Newsmen who had gathered to witness her departure urged her to wait until the heavy winds and snow abated and the dangerous crosscurrents in the river subsided. Lola laughed at them, climbed into the skiff, and pushed off.

The reporters attributed her survival to a near-miracle. Often she disappeared from view. The skiff was in constant danger of capsizing or being rammed by an ice floe, and the winds, combined with the tricky current, made it almost impossible for her to steer the tiny craft. But after a struggle that lasted more than three hours, her recklessness was rewarded and she came ashore at Twentieth Street in Manhattan. Lola was exhausted and her clothes were ruined, but her latest adventure had succeeded and she had proved she could master the elements.

Martin went ahead with his plans to present her in a revival of *Lola Montez in Bavaria,* which he intended to open in late March, but Lola summoned him to her hotel and announced that she had changed her mind. She had made her last appearance as an actress, she said, and henceforth intended to lead a different kind of life. Martin, unable to persuade her to change her mind, was forced to abandon his project.

Lola was in earnest, and it may even be said that the woman who moved to a small boardinghouse on East Ninth Street was a new person. Perhaps her brush with death in the skiff had changed her or deranged her; perhaps her unhappy experiences in Australia were responsible. Whatever the reason, she became a devout convert to what can only be described as her own highly individual brand of Christianity. In it she combined a devout faith in a Protestant God with touches of spiritualism and an almost transcendental mysticism. Cynics of a later period were inclined to believe that she had donned the hair shirt of the penitent sinner.

Whatever her reasons, there could be no doubt that she was sincere, and the reporters who interviewed her accepted her conversion as genuine. Her funds were still ample, yet she moved into cramped quarters and, giving up the many luxuries to which she was accustomed, seemed content to lead a simple life. Having taken wine with her meals since the age of fifteen, she now gave up all alcoholic beverages. For many years a heavy smoker, she would no longer touch cigarettes or cigars. She got rid of the expensive pieces of furniture and bric-a-brac that had been her prized possessions—her two-room apartment resembled a monastic cell.

The change in Lola's appearance was the most dramatic of all. She gave away her finery, took to wearing high-necked, long-sleeved dresses of heavy, shapeless wool, most of them dark gray or dull brown. Her hair, so long her pride, was now parted in the middle, drawn back severely into a bun at the nape of her neck, and unornamented. She no longer used cosmetics, and publicly revealed that she had smashed more than fifty bottles of perfume. She seemed to age overnight and in 1858 suddenly looked far older than her forty years.

She even became indifferent to men—other than the members

of the clergy who advised her in spiritual matters. The Reverend C. Chauncey Burr, a prominent New York minister who was pastor of an interdenominational church, is the authority for her statement that she planned to devote the rest of her life to helping others. "If I can assist just one woman in the avoidance of the pitfalls that made me so miserable," he quoted her as saying, "I shall be happy evermore."

What caused Lola's sudden transformation from glamorous adventuress into near-saint? It is this shift, when seen in depth, that provides a key to her whole, complex character.

To the extent that any of her feelings throughout her life were genuine, her conversion was real. Although she herself claimed, to be sure, that she suddenly saw the "light of God," her reasons were many and complicated; in all probability most of her motivations were unconscious. A number of clues point the way.

The most important of them lead to what is almost certainly an oversimplification of the truth: that Lola finally succumbed to a kind of insanity that had threatened her for so many years. Always abnormally narcissistic, always moving in a dream world of her own creation, she was able to live in accordance with her illusions for more than a decade and a half—because of her great beauty, which must have reached its peak in her twenties or thirties, and because of her almost unbelievable nerve, or courage, which had its roots in her insensitivity to anyone other than herself. The fading of her beauty could easily have been a force strong enough to push her off the cliff of her own creation.

It would be easy to say that Lola long suffered from some form of paranoid manic-depression, which developed from her exceptionally unhappy childhood into a lifelong emotional instability. It is certainly true that, insecure and unwanted, she took refuge in daydreams. As an adult she seemingly made those dreams come true, always playing a role, always posing, always adopting a new and different personality. With Franz Liszt she was the perfect artist's mistress, absorbed in his creative work. With Dujarier she combined sensuality with a love of domesticity she had never before shown and never would again. With King Ludwig she became, for a time, the flaming liberal and during this brief period alone was concerned with political issues and ideals.

Lola remained a perpetual adolescent, and for years lived at least some of her adolescent dreams. She was successful; in part because of her beauty, in part because she played each of her roles with such extraordinary energy and conviction—convinced by her own acting. Throughout these years her conduct frequently approached the dividing line that separated the barely permissible from that which society could not tolerate, but she retained enough balance to stay on the right side of the line.

At some point she drifted across this invisible line without realizing it, her regression into infantile attitudes and behavior spurred by a succession of failures, each more catastrophic than the one that preceded it. Although earlier examples can be found, the first total loss of control was in Australia, at the conclusion of a dismal tour that convinced her the public no longer cared about her. There is virtually no other explanation for her vicious whip duel in a hotel lobby, an act that defies common sense and any human instinct for self-preservation.

The next incident took place in France, where her presence was almost universally ignored. Determined to call attention to herself at almost any cost, she invented her romance with the popular actor Mauclerc. She succeeded in regaining the spotlight momentarily but fled into isolation when Mauclerc gave her back her own and made her the butt of popular ridicule.

Her failure to repeat her success in the United States must be seen as a final, shattering blow, and the publicity stunt she staged on crossing the Hudson River in a frail boat as a frantic gesture made by a desperate woman.

Even if Lola had been able to distinguish her own fictions from reality, her bizarre way of living subjected her to almost unimaginable strains. Changing her entire way of life as rapidly as she changed lovers, remaking herself into the image that the man—or the circumstance—of the moment required, she pulled off one mask to don another with astonishing rapidity. And yet the Bavarian stateswoman, the glamorous stage star, and the pioneer frontierswoman living in the California wilderness were inescapably the same woman.

Never knowing when to stop, Lola played each of her roles to the hilt, throwing herself into each successive part with dazzling abandon. It must not be forgotten either that throughout the years of her greatest triumphs she always wore a *double* mask: no matter what else she might be passing herself off as at the moment, she was nearly always pretending to be of Spanish birth, always speaking with an accent that was unnatural and, presumably, uncomfortable.

In her affairs with Liszt, Dujarier, and Ludwig, not to mention the last three of her four marriages, she never dropped her Spanish pose, and there is no evidence to suggest that any one of her many sophisticated lovers and friends knew she was staging an act. It staggers the imagination to realize how much better an actress she was than her contemporaries knew: even when making love, she kept up her pseudo-Spanish accent!

Behind these façades and fictions—steadying Lola when she went to extremes, restraining her when she was on the verge of losing control—were her unique personality traits. Their effect on her life can best be seen in her imperviousness to criticism. Distinguished theatrical and musical reviewers in Great Britain, America, France, Poland, Bavaria, and Australia condemned her performances with one voice. Almost without exception they wrote that she had no talents as an actress, singer, or dancer, generally damning her stage efforts as caricatures of reality.

A truly sensitive woman would have been crushed by these reactions, in which theatergoers enthusiastically concurred by trying to hiss her off the stage. But Lola seemed to shrug off the attacks of her detractors and blithely continued to play the role of a dancer, actress, and occasional singer.

The astonishing self-confidence that made such a response possible has to have been rooted in her beauty. That, at least, was real. It was, moreover, the foundation on which she built her entire adult life and career. Even the most derogating of her critics had to acknowledge her beauty, and no man, no matter how great his contempt for her, could laugh at Lola when facing her alone.

Whether Lola was as lovely as she and her contemporaries believed or whether she succeeded in creating the illusion of great beauty, becomes a moot question. In conquest after conquest she proved to the world—and to her own satisfaction, which undoubtedly was far more important to her—that she was glamorous beyond compare.

A photograph of Lola taken in 1858, after her conversion, is extraordinarily revealing. Earlier daguerreotypes and paintings show that until her return to the United States from Australia by way of Europe, Lola was a beauty. But this later photograph proves that her perfection of face and figure, whether real or the innermost of her masks, was now destroyed. In the photograph Lola looks like a frump. Her hair, parted in the middle, is pulled taut across hollow, lined cheeks. She sags in her chair, a defeated woman of middle age, and her eyes are dull. Even her hands, demurely crossed in her lap beneath long sleeves, are gnarled, and the high-necked dress cannot conceal the creases in her throat.

At no time in her *Autobiography*, her correspondence, or elsewhere had Lola ever suggested that she, like all human beings, might be subject to the aging process. In her mid-thirties she seemingly looked as fresh, vital, even young, as she had at the height of her beauty; nearing her forties, she must have been aware that she was losing it. Even if her amazing vitality—aided by the careful application of cosmetics—concealed the truth from others, she must have been forced to face reality when she looked into her mirror and saw hair that was losing its luster and tiny lines that formed at the mouth and eyes. Stiff muscles, the exhaustion she undoubtedly felt after violent physical exertions, unquestionably told her the same story.

One could reasonably assume that this awareness may have partially inspired Lola's retirement to the deep forests of California, from which she emerged only when her restless ego demanded the world's attention. If this guess is premature, there can be little doubt that her disastrous Australian tour made her feel unloved and unlovely, and that such feelings helped cause her increasing loss of control. Her unhappy stay in Paris and the cold reception she was accorded thereafter in the United States were the final blows that stripped away the last of the illusions that had sustained her for so many years.

It is possible that facing the truth speeded the disintegration of her beauty, which had so much depended upon the effect Lola exerted on others.

Granting that a change was inevitable, why did Lola change so drastically? In a sense she had no real choice. Her vanity still demanded that she be recognized, admired, even applauded; she still craved the power to move and influence others. Certainly she could have done nothing more dramatic than exchange the black velvet gown of the sinner for the penitent's gown of shapeless wool. The reformed Lola went out on lecture tours, where a new and different audience responded to her.

In one sense Lola had not really changed at all. No longer able to play the kind of role that had been her stock in trade for so long, she discarded it for another, and the reaction she won made the transformation worth her while. Middle-aged and elderly ladies comprised her audience now, and if their applause was less boisterous than that of gold miners, it was equally devoted, equally genuine. If she could not be glamorous, she would be the epitome of sincerity; as always, she went to the extreme.

Those who thought the change in Lola was temporary eventually learned better. She played the penitent with her old energy and a new kind of flamboyance. Believing that she faced a challenge, she was determined to succeed as a righteous woman.

For some months after her overnight conversion, she floundered, however, gradually finding her way back to whatever was genuine in her new convictions. At first she became a member of a sect known as the Christian Spiritualists and attended nightly seances. Later she held long conversations with some of her illustrious predecessors, among them Cleopatra, Madame du Barry, and Mary Queen of Scots, all of whom shared her view that licentiousness caused great sorrow.

Gradually through 1857 Lola edged toward a more conventional approach to life and religion, and by the end of the year she knew what she wanted to do for the rest of her life. She retired to her desk, wrote a series of lectures that were published in late 1858, together with the third and last version of her *Autobiography*, and made it known that she was available for lecture engagements. She had, it would seem, no intention of making a profit from these talks. All she wanted in return was her expenses, and she suggested that a number of church groups in a given city might band together to pay for her transportation, room, and board.

The titles of her lectures were provocative: "Beautiful Women," "Gallantry," "Heroines of History," "The Comic Aspects of Love," "Women of Paris," "Romanism."

If the good ladies who belonged to various church auxiliaries and similar organizations hoped to be titillated by hearing the notorious Lola Montez address them on such fascinating topics, they must have been disappointed. Whatever titles Lola chose for these first lectures, each was no more than an ill-defined sermon that a first-year student in a theological seminary might write. The talks were as lacking in wit as they were in wisdom, and Lola rarely made more than a vague reference or two to her own past.

She mentioned herself only in passing, seldom straying beyond such sentiments as, "One who is qualified to be a happy wife and good mother need never look with envy upon the woman of genius, if genius it be, whose mental powers, by fitting her for the stormy arena of politics, have unfitted her for the quiet walks of domestic life."

Lola's delivery was even deadlier than her material. Letters sent to her by the presidents and secretaries of various church auxiliaries congratulated her on her serenity and remarked at length on her calm. What these women really meant was that

Lola was numbingly dull. At no time in her life had she ever been able to project the force of her remarkable personality across footlights, even when playing the leading role in melodrama—even when playing herself. Her delivery had ever been wooden, her manner stilted, and for many years she had been criticized for betraying a fatal self-consciousness. These faults were exaggerated now, and the few men who accompanied their wives to her talks usually found an excuse to escape into a corridor, where they stayed until she was done.

Nonetheless, the demand for her lectures was so overwhelming that Lola was convinced she had found her true mission. Requests for speaking engagements came to her from dozens of American cities; she tried to honor all of them, traveling without rest in 1858, when she visited virtually every community of appreciable size east of the Mississippi River. She continued to accept no recompense other than her expenses, which must have been one of the reasons she found herself in demand as a speaker.

It cannot be emphasized too strongly that if Lola was playing a new role, she believed in it implicitly. If she indeed was a paranoid manic-depressive, this was the last manic phase of her career and life, and she enjoyed every moment of it. The newspapers no longer devoted front-page space to her activities, but in quiet interviews usually buried in sections devoted to local news, Lola was quoted again and again: she had found her true vocation; her previous suffering had not been in vain; she was content.

Some of the ideas expressed in her lectures were novel. She had no use for the suffragettes who were demanding the right to vote, and insisted that women were too far removed from politics to understand what to do with the franchise. It would be far better, she said, if they remembered they were females. Then they could use feminine wiles to influence the men who held the vote. A woman, she told her audiences, could get anything she wanted in the world if she exerted enough effect on the men in her life.

The women of England, she said in another lecture, were the most beautiful in the world. American women paid too little attention to their appearances, were afraid to utilize their feminine charms, and were inclined to hide in dark corners rather than assert themselves. She liked American men, but they lacked the gallantry every woman loved, principally because they were so practical. They would be far more fascinating if they sometimes forgot and even abandoned their ever-present mercenary goals. But she concluded on a note that pleased her listeners: "Love in the United States is as brave, honest, and sincere a passion as it is elsewhere!"

The lecture on Romanism began as a violent attack on the Roman Catholic Church, but Lola gradually modified it, in part because many of the requests for speaking engagements came to her from Catholic women's groups. By the middle of 1858, she appeared to have lost her hatred of Catholicism, and the published version of her lectures contains no remarks stronger than, "America does not yet recognize how much she owes to the Protestant principle. It has given the world the four great gifts of modern times —steamboats, railroads, telegraphs, and the American Republic!" She made no attempt to explain how any of these boons to mankind had grown out of Protestantism.

In none of Lola's lectures did she mention the issue of slavery that had brought the United States to the brink of a civil war. When asked by various groups to address them on the subject, this woman who had been hailed as a liberal and humanitarian during and subsequent to her stay in Bavaria replied that she was not qualified.

Her lecture tour of 1858 was an unqualified success, and she relished her newly acquired standing as a woman of virtue. Ladies who would have snubbed the preconversion Lola now gave dinner parties in her honor when she visited their cities, and few doors were still closed to her. She displayed no interest in men, even refusing to accept eligible bachelors as escorts, and under no circumstances would she engage in light conversation with the husbands, brothers, or sons of her hostesses. Four husbands and more lovers than she cared to count had been more than enough; at the age of forty, she was finished with men for all time.

Indeed, Lola had not changed. She continued to dream of new conquests, and, having won the New World, sought the admiration of the Old for the reformed Lola Montez who was devoting herself to the instruction of other women. Never having forgotten that she had been rejected and mocked in England, she decided to make another attempt to storm the castle of that first and last enemy.

[CHAPTER XXIV]

Lola laid siege to London in stages rather than making a direct assault on the city. On November 15, 1858, she sailed from New York on the American steamer *Pacific,* landing at Galway on November 23. Seemingly unperturbed by the modesty of her reception, she announced her availability and was immediately booked for several lecture engagements. In this citadel of Irish Catholicism, she made no references to the Church of Rome, and when newspaper reporters asked about her experiences in Bavaria, she carefully refrained from mentioning her conflict with the Jesuits. She had lived four decades before learning the rudiments of tact and diplomacy.

From Galway she went to Dublin, which she had last visited a quarter of a century earlier, and there she repeated her American professional and social triumphs. Still she was afraid to storm London; the Irish were an emotional people, but the chilly English might reject her again.

Continuing the back-door approach, Lola opened her English tour in industrial Manchester, touring from mid-December, 1858 to mid-April, 1859 without respite, visiting such provincial cities as Sheffield, Leicester, Birmingham, Wolverhampton, Worcester, Nottingham, Leamington, and Bristol. The enthusiasm of he audiences mounted as she moved from one place to another, and women who came to gape at her remained to applaud and invite her to their homes for overnight visits. She told them what they wanted to hear and already believed, so she was a success—once again.

A number of ladies from the provinces, having learned that London was Lola's goal, worked together and raised the funds to rent St. James' Hall, one of the largest and most prestigious auditoriums in London. Lola agreed to deliver a talk there on the evening of April 10, 1859, an experience that promised to be the climax of her new public life. Every seat was sold, and many of her friends from the provinces were in the audience. Lola displayed none of her inner turmoil as she walked onto the stage and stood before the lectern. The *Era* of April 10 tells the story:

Madame Lola Montez, parenthetically putting forth her more aristocratic title of Countess of Landsberg, commenced on Thursday evening the first of a series of lectures at the St. James's Hall.

Revisiting this country, she has first felt her footing as a lecturer in the provinces, and now venturing upon the ordeal of a London audience, she has boldly added her name to the list of those who have sought, single-handed, to engage their attention. If any amongst the full and fashionable auditory that attended her appearance fancied, with a lively recollection of certain scandalous chronicles, that they were about to behold a formidable-looking woman of Amazonian audacity, and palpably strong-wristed as well as strong-minded, their disappointment must have been grievous; greater if they anticipated the legendary bear at her side and the traditional pistols in her girdle and the horsewhip in her hand.

The Lola Montez who made a graceful and impressive obeisance to those who gave her on Thursday night so cordial and encouraging a reception appeared simply as a good-looking lady in the bloom of womanhood, attired in a plain grey dress, with easy, unrestrained manners, and speaking earnestly and distinctly, with the slightest touch of a foreign accent that might belong to any language from Irish to Spanish to German.

The subject selected by the fair lecturer was the distinction between the English and the American character, which she proceeded to demonstrate by a discourse that must be pronounced decidedly didactic rather than diverting. With most of the characteristics mentioned as illustrative of each country, we presume the majority of her hearers had, in the course of their reading or experience, become already acquainted. That America looked to the future for her greatness, England to her past; that Americans believed in the spittoon as a valuable institution, and speed as the great condition of success in all things—it hardly needed a Lola Montez to come from the West to inform us. The excitable temperament of our trans-Atlantic brethren, their readiness to raise idols and to demolish them, the great liberty of opinion that there prevails, and the little toleration of its expression, were the leading points of a lecture lasting an hour and a quarter, blended with a compliment to the American ladies, a tributary acknowledgment of the virtues of our own, and a digression into American politics as connected with everything.

There was no attempt to weave into the subject a few threads of personal interest, no mention of any incident that had happened to her, and no anecdote that might have enlivened the dissertation in any way. The lecture might have been a newspaper article, the first chapter of a book of travels, or the speech of a long-winded American ambassador at a Mansion House dinner. All was exceedingly decorous and diplomatic, slightly gilded here and there with those commonplace laudations that stir a British public into the utterance of patriotic plaudits.

A more inoffensive entertainment could hardly be imagined; and when the six sections into which the lady had divided her discourse were exhausted, and her final bow elicited a renewal of the applause that had accompanied her entrance, the impression on the departing visitors must have been that of having spent an hour in company with a well-informed lady who had gone to America, had seen much to admire there, and coming back, had over the tea-table the talk of the evening to herself. Whatever the future disquisitions of the Countess of Landsberg may be, there is little doubt that many will go to hear them for the sake of the peculiar celebrity of the lecturer. But anyone who expects to see a speaker other than a circumspect lady will suffer sore disappointment.

At long last England accepted Lola, according her the respectable status she had always sought. It no longer even mattered to her that in certain circles doors remained closed. She kept a spiritual diary during her sojourn in England; very sincere, very dull. Her diary was intended for no eyes but her own, and in it one theme predominates: she had found the peace she had sought all of her life. There was no need for her to search for new sensations or thrills, to behave outrageously and shock society, to defy conventions. Making no excuses for her past, she refused to rationalize and insisted that she would not look backward.

She remained in England until the late autumn, and her life during this period was uneventful. She lectured from time to time, although newspapers no longer reported on the speeches, and she regularly visited London's East End, where she and a number of her new friends distributed Bibles to the poor. As she indicated in her diary, it pleased her that the world had forgotten her existence, that she could live in her own way now, at peace with all mankind.

The cynics who doubted the depth of her conversion were wrong, but those who claimed her personality made it impossible for her to spend the rest of her days in semi-anonymity were right.

Late in November, 1859, Lola returned to the United States. At her first lecture, delivered two months later in Brooklyn, she appeared in flowing white robes, white shoes and stockings, and a white headgear that bore a suspicious resemblance to a halo. Her audience accepted her costume, and she wore it again in February and March of 1860 on a lecture tour of New England. The Boston newspapers mildly criticized her attire, but the press elsewhere did not comment on her obvious resemblance to the popular concept of an angel.

The content of Lola's lectures changed after her return to the United States, now becoming evangelical. Her new aim was the salvation of other sinners, and her diary is filled with rhetoric on the subject. Late in March of 1860, after her return to New York, she delivered the last of her lectures in Brooklyn. When a local florist and his wife came forward at the end of the talk and addressed her in thick Scottish burrs, she was delighted to discover they were old friends whom she had known in Scotland. Isaac Buchanan had been a neighbor when she had lived with her stepfather's family, and Elna Buchanan had been a classmate.

The friendship was revived, and Lola moved from a modest lodging house in Manhattan to a similar establishment in Brooklyn. Through the influence of the Buchanans, she joined the

Episcopal Church, the first voluntary affiliation of her life with any religious organization.

The Reverend F. L. Hicks, the clergyman who became her spiritual adviser, expressed his own opinion of her conversion when interviewed several years later. "So far as outward actions could show," he said, "with her 'old things' had passed away, and all things had become new. With a heart full of sympathy for the poor outcasts of her own sex, she devoted the last active months of her life to visiting them at the Magdalen Asylum, near New York, warning them and instructing them with a spirit which yearned over them, that they, too, might be brought into the fold."

Most of those who had known Lola throughout the better part of her adult life would not have recognized her as she made her regular visits to the Magdalen Asylum, the first rehabilitation center for prostitutes ever established in New York State. There is no record to indicate that she changed the views or sentiments of any of the inmates confined there, but she threw herself into her work with such energy—according to the Reverend Hicks—that she must have enjoyed herself.

By this time she was less well fixed financially. Although she had disposed of none of her jewelry, her reserves of cash were dwindling. For all practical purposes she had earned no money since her Australian tour, and she was not wealthy enough to live indefinitely on her savings. At the instigation of the Buchanans, she invested what was left of her money in one of the new thrift banks that were springing up around the country.

Nothing in Lola's day-to-day existence resembled the life she had lived for so many years. She was never seen with men, never at the theater, and she rarely ate in any restaurant other than small establishments in Brooklyn where families congregated on Sundays. She saw no friends except the Buchanans and a few fellow workers at her church, and she devoted most of her spare time to reading the Bible and books of Biblical history.

In the early summer of 1860, Lola suddenly became a recluse. She gave up her visits to the streetwalkers she had been trying to reform and left her modest lodgings only to attend church services. According to the Buchanans and the Reverend Hicks, she was convinced she had contracted consumption and would soon die. Two physicians examined her at various times during the summer, principally because the Buchanans insisted, but neither could find any trace of such a disease. Still Lola persisted in her belief.

Food now meant so little to Lola that she no longer went marketing; she would have starved, had Elna Buchanan not brought baskets to her apartment. When she attended church, she appeared in clothing as shabby as it was drab, and no one seemed able to arouse her from her lethargy. At the end of July, when the Reverend Hicks tried to cajole her into leading a more active life, Lola allegedly said to him, "What does it matter? In another six months I'll be dead, and it will serve me right."

In September she lost so much weight that Elna Buchanan suspected—correctly—that she was no longer cooking any of the food brought to her. Lola's girlhood friend started cooking the meals herself, bringing them each day to Lola's lodgings. Lola regained some of the weight she had lost, but there was no improvement in her spirits.

Politics did not interest her, and she was indifferent to the Presidential election of 1860 which split the country. Others regarded the election of Abraham Lincoln as a guarantee that the United States would soon be plunged into a civil war, but Lola neither knew nor cared. She had now given up all of her reading, and whenever the Buchanans or the Reverend Hicks visited her, they found her seated in a chair before a dirt-streaked window that overlooked a small backyard vegetable garden. As nearly as they could judge, Lola did nothing but stare into space.

Her health declined, and on January 10, 1861, not yet forty-three years old, she suffered a stroke that left her partly paralyzed. The Buchanans hired a nurse to attend her and spent hours each day at her apartment, but neither they nor the physicians they summoned were able to persuade her that she had a good chance to recover. Early on the morning of January 17, Lola died in her sleep.

She was buried two days later in Greenwood Cemetery, Brooklyn, with the Reverend Hicks conducting the graveside service. The Buchanans and nine unidentified mourners attended. Perhaps no one thought of notifying the press; no newspaper in the Old World or the New carried the story of Lola's death.

In accordance with the instructions written in her own hand three months earlier in a will, her gravestone bore a simple inscription:

MRS. ELIZA GILBERT

Born 1818 Died 1861

Lola left the sum of $1,000 to the Buchanans as a token payment for the many kindnesses they had shown her. She left the rest of her estate, which amounted to approximately $12,000, to "the poor who are poor also in spirit," directing that the Reverend Hicks dispense the money as he saw fit.

Not until several years later when the news of Lola's death gradually spread through preoccupied, war-torn America and drifted across the Atlantic, did it finally occur to certain newspaper editors that the disposition of her jewelry collection was not known. Concerted efforts were made by the New York *Tribune*, the London *Herald*, and *La Presse* in Paris to find out what had become of it.

According to the last estimates, which had been made just before Lola's departure for Australia, her jewelry was worth something in excess of half a million dollars. All of the gems, if taken from their settings, could have been sold without difficulty. When reporters went to the Buchanans for interviews, they denied any knowledge of the fortune. In later years the claim was made by several of Lola's biographers that Elna Buchanan had stolen the collection, presumably during Lola's last days when she was very ill. The sensational story was an appropriate final chapter in the life of Lola Montez, but like so much that preceded it, no evidence was forthcoming. If the Buchanans were guilty, they certainly did not enjoy the benefits of the theft: they continued to live modestly, working hard, and when they died in the late 1870's, they each left small estates.

According to another of the many theories on the subject, Lola herself cashed in the jewels, one by one, in order to support herself during the last years of her life. It must be remembered that she earned no income during her lecture tours, and that she paid for the printing of the final version of her *Autobiography*, combined with her lectures, out of her own purse. It would seem all but impossible, however, for her to spend and give away a half-million dollars over a period of less than six years.

The mystery, unsolved to the present day, kept her in the public eye for a time, which surely would have delighted Lola Montez. In death as in life, she was the subject of rumor, speculation, and gossip. Had the disappearance of her gems been deliberate, Lola could not have planned a more suitable memorial.

"To be adored"

"There's a lesson in here somewhere"
(to be learned)

"People who should Know"

"Just another Man"

"(Gentle) Men of the Regiment"